SILO KILLER
(Qu'est ce que c'est?)

Jonathan Evans

Silo Killer Qu'est ce que c'est?
First published 2024 by LEED in conjunction with Tangent Books

LEED
25 Burghley Road
Bristol
BS6 5BL
lloydevanslts@btinternet.com

Tangent Books
31 Balmain Street
Bristol
BS4 3DB
www.tangentbooks.co.uk

ISBN 9798328734677

Author: Jonathan Evans
Typsetting: Robert Attwood
Cover Design: Joe Burt
Copyright: Jonathan Evans

Jonathan Evans has asserted his right under the Copyright Design And Patents Act of 1968 to be identified as the author of this work. This book may not be reproduced or transmitted in any form or by any means without the prior written consent of the publisher, except by a reviewer who wishes to quote brief passages in connection with a review written in a newspaper or magazine or broadcast on television, radio or on the Internet.

A CIP record of this book is available at the British Library

Author's note

The 'Ndrangheta and the Victoria market wars

The 'Ndrangheta, known more simply as the Mafia to most Australians, has controlled Italian-Australian organised crime along the east coast of Australia since the early 20th century. The 'Ndrangheta began in Queensland, where its base was in in the fruit and vegetable industry.

The notorious Market Wars were a vicious struggle for control over Melbourne's Victoria Market and lasted, intermittently, from the mid-1960s until the late 1980s. The wars began in 1962 after the death of Melbourne godfather Domenico 'The Pope' Italiano, followed several weeks later by the death of the enforcer Antonio 'The Toad' Barbera, both of natural causes. Recent reports suggest that the Melbourne Mafia is still heavily involved in both fruit and vegetable distribution and the drugs trade.

Prologue

Rainbow is a small, dry place with a population of about five hundred people, located in the north of Victoria about six hours from Melbourne in a region known as the Mallee. It became established at the turn of the twentieth century at a site known as Rainbow Rise, named after a crescent sand dune which, after a local shower, was temporarily covered with wildflowers. I guess this was at the time the wheat lands were being opened up, because the dune was located where the grain silos stand today.

The Mallee is the sort of region where conversations always turn around rainfall. "They had two points last night at Hopetoun", or "Wycheproof had a shower", were the sort of things you would hear at the Eureka Pub or in the town's shop whilst waiting to be served. It is the hottest and driest part of the state. I kid you not, I've seen rain falling out of the sky which never reached the ground. I've also known farmers commit suicide when the rain they expected failed to materialise.

It was late January 1984 when I first arrived there, the drought was in full swing and I had no idea then that I was about to take the first step into an adventure that would take me, in fear of my life, halfway across a continent.

Chapter 1:
The great map of Bill Badcock

It still comes to me sometimes in my dreams, startling in size and almost incomprehensible.

When I first saw it, sure, I was worried. Who wouldn't be? Just try putting yourself in my shoes and see how you'd feel.

I had gone there in response to a letter from the Education Department to discuss my posting. Back in the UK, several months before, I'd had an amiable interview and been sold the delights of working 'down under'. I dimly remember asking about where I'd be located and being offered a typically Aussie response: "No worries mate, we'll sort you out when you get there."

I'd taken them at their word, so here I was, waiting to be sorted out.

Bill Badcock's office was on the second floor, his name on a board outside the door. Badcock, I thought to myself. I'd known kids at school called Allcock, Mycock, Jaycock and Geecock, but Badcock? That really was something, and I knew I might have difficulty getting my mouth around it when it came to introductions.

I knocked on the door and entered. I needn't have worried. A burly bloke aged about forty and sporting a Dennis Lillie moustache stood up smartly and introduced himself with almost indecent haste.

"Badcoe's the name, call me Bill."

I was relieved and grateful.

"Welcome to Godzone, Tom. How're you settling in?"

"Just fine," I replied, "I'm living with mates in Glen Iris."

"So, I guess you're wanting to find out about the new school?"

"Yeah," I said. "They told me in London that it would be a city school and I was kind of hoping that it might be somewhere in the Eastern suburbs."

Bill shifted uneasily.

"Well, we haven't quite managed to sort something out for you in town, but we've got you a job in a beaut little place called Rainbow. You'll love it."

Rainbow? RAINBOW? I'd never heard of it! Where was it? I was afraid that it might be some faceless suburb up in the northern reaches of the city, a bit like Doncaster. That would be bloody awful. It sounded like a piece of shit real estate just like Sunshine or Tottenham, an hour out and boring as hell; all rusting railyards and decaying chemical plants or, even worse, new urban sprawl, shopping malls and car parks. Please God, tell me it isn't so.

I needed some more details.

"Where exactly is Rainbow?" I asked. Bill didn't answer immediately; he looked away for a second and his Adam's apple seemed to do a swallow dive. He cleared his throat, "I'm not really sure, but I think it's somewhere in the Mallee."

In the Mallee? Jesus H fucking Christ, the Mallee? that's hundreds of miles from anywhere.

"Come on, I'll show you," Bill said, noticing that the colour had drained from my cheeks. He led me upstairs to a large high-ceilinged room lined with tall library shelves and containing Victorian map cases, all brown polished wood, looking as though nothing had been disturbed for about fifty years. It was quiet. Bill strode briskly in and opened a map drawer at random. He was searching for something. "Not in here," he said. His eyes began scanning the top of the high walls around the room. Here there were place names painted in black, on white ground. I guessed that the artwork dated from around the

1890s and identified different parts of the state. I remember seeing *Gippsland*, *Cann River*, *Western Districts*, *Port Campbell* and then, standing proudly, at the end of the row, *The Mallee*. "Here it is," said Bill and proceeded to haul on a hefty rope that hung from the ceiling. As he pulled, an enormous roll map descended. It must have been about thirty feet high and about fifteen feet wide. Bearing the legend *The Mallee 1915*, it was almost totally blank. However, near the top were a couple of light blue areas which I assumed were lakes. I could also see a black spidery line running across the map which I knew was a railway. There were two roads, and almost nothing else.

We both looked at the map. Where was Rainbow?

"It's here somewhere," said Bill. He conjured up a long, pointed stick and started waving it vaguely at the map. He was talking to himself. "Mm, let's see." After a few moments he walked to the other side of the room and wheeled over an unusual contraption, a set of stepladders on wheels. Bill rolled this to the base of the map and climbed up for a closer inspection. "Ah, here it is. You beauty!" He pointed to a spot in the middle of nowhere. "That's it Tommo, Rainbow."

I stared and, for once in my life, was speechless for a few seconds, and then just about managed to utter a single word. "Oh."

Bill seemed pleased at my enthusiasm. "There's a couple of lakes" he said, "and I think one of 'em's got water in."

"Don't they normally have water in?"

"Nah, Lake Albacutya has been dry since about 1949, but I'm pretty sure the other one's wet. At least, it was last year." There was a pause, and I wondered if he knew that I knew that he knew this wasn't quite the location I was hoping for. After a few seconds he carried on, "I can tell that you're really going to love this place, Tommo." Bill beamed. I was not so sure, and my stomach began cramping at the prospect. "Come on, I'll find some more information."

We went into another room lined with bookshelves. Bill pulled down an enormous tome. It had a red leather cover and bore the inscription, *State Gazetteer, 1954, Vol XXIII, The Mallee*.

"Here we are, page 527, Rainbow." Bill showed me the entry. It gave me all the information I needed. It didn't exactly say it was hotter than the surface of the sun but, reading between the lines, that was what it meant. It also seemed like the sort of place that might strongly attract fugitives from the law, or people who had an aversion to the twentieth century. I also figured that it was about five hundred miles in any direction from anywhere interesting.

There was another strained silence.

Bill must have noticed my discomfort.

"Everybody who goes there seems to love it," he said.

"Really?"

"Well, I figure they must, as they all seem to stay there. They never write back and ask for a transfer, so I reckon they get on just fine."

I thought to myself, what you mean is they go there, and you never hear from them again.

By the time I walked out of the building and back onto Collins Street I was already planning my escape.

Chapter 2:
Astral weeks

When I got back to Trev and Steph's from my meeting with Bill Badcock, I was still in a state of shock.

As I walked along Florence Street I passed manicured lawn after manicured lawn until I came to what looked like a jungle, where a single storey house was almost completely hidden in dense shade by thick bush and tall gum trees.

It was just after noon, and the sun was at its zenith as I ploughed my way through the long, dry grass to the front door. Steph told me that the neighbours had complained that the lot was a fire risk, and I must admit I had to agree.

The front door was slightly ajar and so I wandered in. As I did, I noticed how deliciously cool and dark it was, so dark in fact that I had difficulty seeing. Despite the hour, music was blaring out from the living room and in the gloom, as my eyes began to adjust, I could see the vague shape of a body sprawled across a chaise longue. Trev was lying in state, listening to Captain Beefheart at full throttle.

Ever since I had come back to Melbourne, Steph had been worrying about Trev's mental health. For the past few years, he had been running a one-man crusade aimed at liberating strays from the various dog pounds around the city but having narrowly avoided being maimed by a particularly fierce hell hound, he had retired from this. This had left him at a bit of a loose end, dabbling in various unusual pastimes. I guess that helps to explain why he had just spent a couple of months up country with a guy called Graham who lived in some old mine workings out towards Bendigo. Graham seemed to have somehow acquired a near monopoly on the southern hemisphere's dope supplies and was working his way through about half a hundredweight of Mullumbimby Madness. A side effect of his hobby had been a preoccupation with star gazing, to which the clear Bendigo skies lent themselves perfectly. Adding some local mushrooms to his diet he had, as a result of his interest in astronomy, successfully established contact with aliens who had abducted him and subjected him to numerous, and not altogether unpleasant, experiments, after which they had conferred upon him the ability to travel through time and space by means of astral projection. They also accorded him the honour of being their ambassador to the human race. One night, after rather a lot of stimulants, Graham had confided all of this to Trev and tried to recruit him to the cause.

Trev, at the time, was doing his own pharmacological research and, for lack of anything better to do, decided to up sticks and head for Bendigo to find out more. Things had gone swimmingly for a while despite the fact that Trev never met any aliens but, as the dope started to run out and Graham talked more and more about his role in the assassination of President Kennedy, Trev began to get disillusioned, and decided to make his excuses and leave.

The experience, however, had left some interesting side effects. Ever since his return, Trev had been having a series of vivid dreams and was convinced that, with the right preparation, he could put himself into a trance and travel across the universe by astral planing.

He had not yet perfected the technique but had been to Camberwell library where he had managed to find a book on the subject, *The Theory and Practice of Astral Projection*, which lay open on the table.

Trev looked done in. "Had the most amazing experience last night, I went to see my brother."

"I thought he lived in England?"

"He does. I was astral planing. I saw him. He was at work, but he couldn't see me."

"Was that it? Did you try to go anywhere else?" I asked.

"I went everywhere, flew over the Amazon rainforest, went to Bali, and ended up at an outback sheep farm talking to a dog I'd rescued. Shit knows why I went there." Trev seemed lost in thought. "Shit," he said, Trev liked this word, "I should have left a message for my brother. Maybe I'll phone him and ask if he noticed anything unusual yesterday."

I thought that the chances of Trev phoning his brother were rather remote, for one thing calls were really expensive – about $10 a minute – for another, I had never seen Trev use a phone.

There was a long pause.

"Where's Steph?" I asked. I couldn't really listen to much more of this.

She was there in the back garden drinking a cup of herbal tea and painting. Steph had arrived in Australia as a baby shortly after the war and was a true 1960s spirit.

She smiled as she saw me, and asked how I was.

I told her about Rainbow.

She listened carefully and then said gently, "You might like it, it's probably really peaceful."

From inside the house came a bellow, "Bullshit, it'll be fucking awful. Why don't you just stay here and live with us?" Trev was listening in.

I must admit the idea of staying in Glen Iris was quite appealing, but I wasn't sure what the Australian Immigration Department would say. My visa was dependent on me working as a teacher, and if I decided to become an astral planing hippy they might not look too kindly on my continued residence in Godzone country.

A couple of days later Trev told me an unusual story. I'd got back there in the early evening. No one answered the front door, so I wandered round the side of the house. Trev was sitting in the back garden.

"I had the most amazing journey last night. I was asleep, and then suddenly I was floating above the world. I could see Steph in the back garden talking to her friend Annie. They were discussing an exhibition in Melbourne and talking about horse riding on the Bogong High Plains. I listened for a while and decided that when I woke up I'd check out with them whether what I'd seen had actually happened. I then decided to go travelling somewhere else.

"I floated down the street to Ted's milk bar. The place had about four customers and supplies were being delivered. It was all quite chaotic and folks were getting frazzled. There was a sales rep there as well, and he was trying to get Ted to accept some paperback books for sale and was manhandling a metal carousel which he put on the counter and began stacking with books. As I watched all this, I had an idea. Either I was dreaming, or I was really astral planing. If I really was there, perhaps I could do something that Ted would remember. I looked at the carousel. It was perched quite precariously on the edge of the counter. Just one push, I thought, and I could tip it over.

"Ted was going frantic. Things were getting out of hand. He was trying to deal not only with the customers, but with deliveries and the sales rep all at the same time. The last thing he needed was a paranormal experience, but that's exactly what I decided to give him. In my astral form I moved to the carousel and pushed it. Nothing happened. I tried again, same result. Nothing. I then concentrated really, really hard. I focused all my energy and pushed with all my strength. The carousel fell to the floor, scattering books everywhere. Ted went ballistic, the place was in chaos. Success! I knew that Ted would remember this. All I had to do when I woke up was to go to the milk bar and ask if the incident with the carousel had actually happened. If it had, I'd been astral projecting and if it hadn't, it was just a dream."

I looked at Trev. "What did you do? Did you check it out?"

"Yeah. First I spoke to Steph and she said that Annie had been around and that they had sat in the back garden and talked about heaps of things, including the stuff that I'd heard. Steph thought I was on to something, but I wasn't certain – you see, I could perhaps have overheard them while I was asleep, so I decided to talk to Ted. I had a cup of tea and wandered down to the milk bar. It was a lot tidier than when I had seen it earlier."

"What about the books? Were they there?"

"Yeah, they were there all right, on the counter in the carousel just like I had seen them before. Ted seemed relatively relaxed.

"I asked Ted what sort of day he had had. He said it'd been a bit of a bugger. In fact he was absolutely Jeffed. Chaos had reigned all morning and, to add insult to injury, some drongo had come in trying to sell him a load of paperback books. Ted didn't really want them, but there was so much on his plate at the time that he just took them."

"Did you ask him?"

"What?"

"About the books? Did the carousel topple over?"

Trevor looked at me. "No," he said, "something stopped me asking. I sort of felt embarrassed, and maybe a little part of me didn't really want to know after all."

"You didn't ask?"

"No."

I couldn't believe this. Even I was beginning to sort of believe in this astral projection thing. There was only one thing to do so I said, "Hold on, why don't I go and see?"

I left the house, turned into Florence Street and was soon on Glen Iris Road.

As I approached the milk bar, I noticed a small crowd gathered on the pavement as someone was being loaded into a waiting ambulance.

"Closed, mate," someone said.

"What's up?" I asked.

"Dunno, he's going to hospital."

Someone else chipped in. "Yeah, fell over that new book thing. He only got it today but. Reckon it fell off the counter when he wasn't looking and tripped him over. He's broken his leg or something."

Was fate determined to prevent me from discovering the truth about astral planing? Had the accident happened because I was trying to break some mystic taboo? Deep down I felt it was wrong to tempt fate, much the same way Trev had felt, and somehow I knew Trev wouldn't be too disappointed that I had failed to provide conclusive proof of his travels through the space time continuum. This belief was reinforced more strongly by the fact that, when I got back, Trev was already on to a new project. He had a book about Einstein which he had bought from the local op shop and was engaged in something he called a 'thought experiment' which involved three bottles of port.

The evening went downhill from there but, thankfully, for a few hours, thoughts of Bill Badcock, the map and Rainbow were banished from my mind.

Chapter 3:
Rainbow

It was late January, and the mercury must have registered about forty-five degrees when the Southern Cross pulled into Horsham station. I immediately felt the furnace from the platform as I stepped down from my carriage. Most folks on the train were heading to Adelaide, and I was the only person who got off. No one got on.

The light was blinding. I squinted and shaded my eyes and there, sheltering from the sun in the deepest recess by the exit, was the Principal's wife, Joan O'Brien. She greeted me with a smile and a delicate handshake. I couldn't help but notice that, despite the heat, she was wearing a pair of thin white gloves, the sort of accessory you would see in pre-war movies.

As we walked out from the station building nothing was moving. There was no breath of wind. No one else was about. There was just us, the car park and the heat.

Joan said briskly that we had a way to go so we'd best make a move. I was okay with that. Sweat was already trickling down my body as I loaded my bags into the car. Anyway, there was nothing I needed in town nor, looking at the shops, was there anything that I could possibly want, unless of course I was out of sheep worming tablets, phosphate fertiliser or parts for my combine harvester.

As we drove north, Joan embarked on a detailed description of the major tourist attractions on offer, displaying especial enthusiasm for the world-renowned rabbit-proof fence which, she reckoned, folks came from as far away as Birchip to see. She was particularly keen that I visit this marvel and, being polite and mildly interested, I agreed. While we chatted, Joan also prepared me for some of the other delights of the area, including the grain terminus, the stockyards, the hill at Wycheproof, and Lakes Hindmarsh and Albacutya. The latter was, unfortunately, dry, as was often the case, but nevertheless not to be missed.

As we approached Jeparit, Joan began to get more and more enthusiastic about the rabbit-proof fence. She knew how many miles of wire were used, the number of fence posts and metal staples, and the cost per mile of this magnificent construction. Sure, you might not be able to see it from the moon, but it was darned impressive. We pulled off the main road, drove for a few minutes to the east and drew up alongside a ragged line of wire netting with holes in it big enough to drive a truck through. At intervals of about ten yards were ancient wooden posts to which the fence was loosely attached. In any other climate everything would have turned to dust long ago, but not here. The fence itself, though rusted and scorched, was still upright. It evoked a bygone era in which the Mallee wheat farmers believed they could conquer nature, while their dreams were haunted by hordes of invading zombie rabbits.

"I bet you've never seen anything like this," Joan said proudly.

"No," I answered weakly, "I don't think I have."

She waited expectantly. Was I supposed to do something? "Do you have a camera? I'll take a picture of you in front of it."

I dug out my Olympus, showed Joan how to use it and smiled grimly as she pressed the shutter.

A few miles along, the town of Jeparit passed like a mirage. It was there one minute and lost behind us in the heat haze the next. I see it in my mind's eye, a single street, enormously wide, occupied by a small number of shops, each with a large veranda to provide shade for prospective patrons. There were no people on the street. It was way too hot for that. The main building was the Hindmarsh Hotel which had several cars parked outside, sun glinting on their polished surfaces. I learnt later that in the old days this pub was frequented by 'Iron Bob' Menzies, a former Prime Minister of Australia, but, of course, he was long gone to the cooler climes of Canberra and beyond.

North of Jeparit, the Mallee stretched on and on, pegged out like an endless, waterless, inland sea.

The first signs I saw of Rainbow were the gigantic wheat silos glinting in the distance. The farms here are huge, and they have to be. There is so little rainfall that they practice dry farming. The acreage is ploughed and left fallow for two years so what little rain may fall can be stored in the soil. Every third year, wheat is planted. Because the properties are so large, and the acreage is so vast, this region provides huge quantities of wheat.

As we rolled into town I saw a patch of dusty ground on the right-hand side, worn bare and surrounded by a barbed wire fence. Inside the fence sat an ancient white caravan beside a tall pole flying the Union Jack.

"We'll just pick up Bill," Joan said. "He runs up the flag when he needs a lift to the pub."

I got out and opened a gate. Three or four large, ugly dogs raced towards me.

"Settle down, yer flamin' mongrels!" came a shout. Bill was sitting in his wheelchair yelling at the beasts that protected him. He rolled up to the car, levered himself upright and leaned against it while I folded his wheelchair and put it into the boot. "Bill," he said, introducing himself, offering a thick, leathery hand once we were on board.

"Tommo," I replied. "Good to meet you."

Bill had been a star footballer for Rainbow in his youth, and tragically had both of his legs blown off during World War Two. Some folks said it happened somewhere on the Kokoda trail; others said it was in Malaya. Whatever the case, everyone agreed Bill was lucky to be alive. When he returned home, he was rightly regarded as a hero and everyone looked out for him. If he ever needed anything, all he had to do was to raise his flag and any passing local would pick him up.

Virtually a mirror image of Jeparit, Rainbow was a conundrum. Much of it clearly belonged to a bygone age, although some of the uglier parts, including the Golden Nugget Motor Inn, were much more recent. My favourite was an old store with a corrugated iron roof, and a wooden door sporting the sign *NH Mathews, COR Agent* which looked as though it had just been dropped in from about 1915. The signage, although faded by the sun, was still bright, and elegant white cursive lettering on a dark blue ground was clearly legible.

REGO FRUIT JELLY CRYSTALS covered one half of the building, whilst the other sported **REGO SELF-RAISING FLOUR**. As I looked at it, I could almost hear the young lads whistling *Tipperary* as they marched past it on the road to Gallipoli.

Bill needed to go to the Eureka Hotel, one of three pubs in town that had not once, since his return, accepted payment for his beer. We dropped him off, but not before he had invited me for a drink later on.

I got out at a small bungalow just off the Jeparit to Hopetoun road. My host, Ross, was a teacher at the school, and he had offered to put me up until I found somewhere to live.

He spoke warmly about the town and impressed upon me how much people were going to rely on me. I began to feel uncomfortable. Already I'd formed the impression that the folks around here were really kind and friendly, and were at pains to make me feel at home. I guess that would've been okay were it not for the fact that the huge openness of the country, the vast distances between towns and the total lack of the trappings of city life combined to make me feel quite ill at ease.

Ross extracted a couple of tinnies from the fridge and handed one to me. "Get this down yer neck mate and be quick about it, we've got a barbie to go to."

We spent the afternoon in the sun, downing beers and eating snags round at the Principal's house near the stock yards. To begin with everyone was on their best behaviour wanting, I guess, to make a good impression. People were being ultra polite but, after a few beers, things relaxed and I began to map out the territory.

Most folks had been in town for some time.

A guy wearing a seersucker jacket, fawn slacks and a Tommy Lawton haircut sidled up and introduced himself. Morris had arrived from the UK twenty years earlier, met a local girl, settled down and got married. From what I gathered he felt as though he was in paradise and couldn't conceive of moving back to the city, let alone the UK.

Ross had been born in Castlemaine and had similarly been seduced by the laid-back friendliness of Rainbow. He had arrived at about the same time as Morris and had his sights on eventually taking over as Principal. Miss Seif was a physics teacher. She didn't say a great deal and I figured that she had a hard time fitting in, but nevertheless she had been there for years. The only newcomers were myself and Andrew, a newly qualified biology teacher from Melbourne. Andrew was excited at the prospect of spending time in the Mallee, and from the get-go I could see that he was going to be there for the long haul.

As the beers went down, the atmosphere became less and less inhibited.

Baz Hardman, a red nosed drinker who was the coach of the local football team, sidled up. For those who don't know, Aussie rules is like a cross between rugby and trench warfare, only much more violent. "You're a Pom, right?"

"That's right."

"How long've you been here?"

"About a month."

"So, you won't have had a bath yet?" Baz chortled at his own joke.

Everyone went quiet, waiting to see how I reacted.

"No," I replied, "we Poms never have baths."

Baz nodded.

"Do you know why we never have baths?"

Baz looked puzzled. "Because you keep coal in the bath?" he said triumphantly.

"Yes, and do you know why we keep coal in the bath?"

"No," Baz said slowly, fearing a trap.

"Because the coal houses are full of fucking Australians."

It was out of my mouth before I could stop myself. I looked around. The chatter of conversation had stopped, and everyone seemed to be gazing downwards as if searching for the entrance to the Rainbow to London tunnel.

Baz burst into laughter, "Bloody Poms," he drawled, "have another beer Tommo."

I downed another cold one and the hum of conversation started up again.

"You've got a way with language. Fancy teaching a bit of Shakespeare?" - this from Morris – "We need someone to do Macbeth for the HSC class."

I thought that this might be a bit beyond me as I was a science teacher, but I was persuaded that, as I was English, I would be fine; besides which, the verb 'to do' probably covered a multitude of potential sins.

Towards evening, Baz made his way back over to me. "It's Jeparit next month." I looked puzzled.

"Jeparit," he repeated. "Big game."

I nodded, none the wiser.

"How do you fancy trying out for the front pocket?" I was still clueless but, having drunk a lot, I smiled in a non-committal way.

Baz clinked my glass, "Great, see you at training tomorrow. Seven o'clock, and, er,...have a bath."

I was still laughing when Ross, who had been observing this, rolled up. "You're in."

"In what?"

"The team. Against Jeparit, the bastards. Broke my arm last time. Pete did his knee; he's never played since. This year we're going to murder them."

Oh Christ, I had been in town only half a day and already I was the new football star, the great hope in the annual grudge match against the most violent thugs the Mallee could muster. In addition, I was an acclaimed Shakespearean guru and had established an unenviable reputation for foul language and poor bodily hygiene.

It had been a long day, and I was ready to go and lie down when Pete Rawlings, the maths teacher and ex Rainbow footballer, limped over. "Coming to the pub? It's horse racing night. You gotta see it Tommo," he grinned.

My heart sank. I realised that there was no way out of this, and so I ended the evening at the Eureka Hotel.

Although Rainbow only has a population of about five hundred people, around half of them seemed to be in the pub. Horse racing night was obviously a big deal.

Most of the blokes were in the back room and were having a fine old time, yelling odds and arguing about form. Bill was perched at the bar and, as I entered, he nodded across to me.

A guy wearing a beer stained Mental as Anything singlet was the bookie. "I'm Grant," he drawled. "Who are you having in race one?"

Now, I have almost no interest in horses, but I did recognise some of the names as they had figured in a broadcast of the Inter Dominion Handicap that I had seen a few weeks earlier. One in particular stood out.

"I'll have five bucks on Gammalite." I passed the money over. Grant gave me a stub and handed me the race card for the rest of the night.

As I studied the runners, a pot of beer was placed in my hand. "From Bill," someone said. Bill nodded and raised his glass.

From somewhere a bugle blew. The landlord made sure we all had plenty of beer and then the video recorder was fired up. The TV monitor was propped above the bar and we watched as the runners and riders came under starter's orders. Sure enough, it was a re-run of the Inter Dominion and, not surprisingly, Gammalite romped home at five to one despite the TV set being attacked by an almost continuous rain of missiles from four furlongs out.

I collected my winnings and stood a round of beers, then up came the second race. I didn't have a clue about this one but, flushed with success, put all my money on number seven. Incredibly, it led the field from start to finish through a storm of cans and bottles accompanied by animal roaring from the crowd.

I can't really remember what happened during the rest of the evening, indeed the fact that I managed to get home in one piece was little short of miraculous. As I collapsed on to my bed, I dimly recall a song running through my brain, something the blokes in the bar had been singing at the end of the night, something I just couldn't get out of my mind. I think it was about Aussie rules football and all I could recall was the chorus: 'Up there Cazaly'.

It had been a long day.

Chapter 4:
Cauliflower

I woke with a terrible headache and about a kilo of loose change and damp five dollar notes in my trouser pockets.

After breakfast I wandered into town and was stunned by a cobalt sky which I imagine could, under certain conditions, make you want to thrash paint all over a canvas or sever your ear. There was no breath of wind and it was already hot as I entered the main store to buy a few bits and pieces. Although the choice was limited, I managed to find most things. I wandered up to the till and placed my shopping on the counter.

"You'll be Tommo then. I'm Stan." Stan was a tall, thin man with dark hair, and skin the colour and texture of a leather wallet. I assumed that he owned the place. "You know your horse flesh, don't you?"

Obviously, news travels fast in Rainbow. I grimaced, "Not really, just beginner's luck."

Stan was referring to my purple streak at last night's video horse racing at the Eureka Hotel. I could vaguely remember the final race ending in a hail of debris accompanied by a bloke blowing on a bugle; and then a wodge of cash being thrust into my hands.

The store was like a living museum. Its centrepiece was the till, a work of art, silver and magnificently ornate. It was, however, unusual in one respect. Each key had a piece of cardboard stuck to it and each piece of cardboard had a number written in green marker pen. I was intrigued.

The till still registered prices in pounds, a currency which had not been in use in those parts since the sixties. Stan rang in my purchases.

My yoghurt (one dollar thirty-nine) came up as seventeen shillings and sixpence ha'penny; shampoo at a dollar ninety-nine rang in at two pounds six and eightpence. The grand total appeared as twenty-seven pounds three shillings and fourpence.

Stan picked up an enormous board about a yard square. It had a complicated grid written on it and the grid was full of numbers.

Stan ran his fingers across. "That will be eight dollars fifty, Tommo," he said. I wondered how that worked but, as Stan seemed as honest as the day was long, I knew that the thought of cheating anybody would have never crossed his mind. As I paid, I noticed that Stan was looking at me in an odd way. He asked me a question I'll never forget. "How are you fixed for the mongrels?"

Now there's a question. "How are you fixed for the mongrels?" I don't know whether you've ever been asked that; I certainly hadn't and was at a loss for an answer.

I thought for a moment that 'the mongrels' might be a local euphemism for some kind of embarrassing infection, before I realised that Stan was actually referring to the forthcoming footy game against the old enemy, the Jeparit Bulldogs. I dimly recalled my conversation with Pete Rawlins and, despite the heat, I shivered and swiftly changed the subject.

I mentioned how impressed I was by the till. I was even more impressed when Stan told me it was nearly a hundred years old. He must've noticed something in my reaction to its age because a faraway look came into his eyes. He took a breath, paused and asked, "Do you want to buy some braces?" I didn't, but Stan wasn't taking no for an answer. He led me out to the back, into a large storeroom, one side of which was shelved from floor to ceiling. Each shelf was stacked with piles of objects wrapped in yellowing tissue paper. They looked like slabs of bacon. He lifted a package down and handed it to me. I unwrapped it. It contained a pair of cream-coloured braces with dark brown leather tabs. Each pair was emblazoned with the legend 'AIF Australian Imperial Forces'. They were magnificent, but I still didn't want braces. "You can have these for a dollar," Stan said. "I've got heaps. My grandfather bought them, army surplus, in 1919."

I stared. There must've been at least ten thousand pairs, enough braces to support the Sydney Harbour Bridge. "How many of these do you sell a week?" I asked.

"Not many. Sold a pair last year but."

I felt rather sorry for Stan and gave him a dollar and walked back out into the sun with my purchases in a small plastic bag.

I headed up Anzac Street towards the bank to open an account. On my way I saw the bugler from the previous evening outside the greengrocer's unloading produce from the back of a large truck. His name was Mario, and he was a hefty man with tufts of what looked like carpet sprouting from inside his singlet. "G'day Tommo," he called from across the street and waved for me to come over. "Here, have this for the Missus." He proffered a large marrow.

I explained that I wasn't married.

He grinned. "Here, take this instead," and handed me a cauliflower. "You wanna come to Melbourne Thursday night?"

"Can't, I'm teaching on Friday."

"Pull a sickie mate – they all do it. Listen," he said in a lower voice, "you and me, we'll leave here at seven, get to town about midnight. Then we'll go to Moonee Ponds, have a few beers, see some prostitutes, then go to Victoria market, pick up the fruit and veg and come home. You'll like it."

I winced.

Then he whispered, "Do not tell Allegra, she'll fucking kill me if she finds out."

I assumed, correctly, that Allegra was his wife. I also assumed that Mario's 'business trips' to Melbourne were Rainbow's worst kept secret. "No, sorry, I can't."

"OK Tommo, you say 'no' now, but wait two, three weeks – you will come – and you'll get more than a cauliflower." He laughed and patted my back.

As I waited in the queue at the Commonwealth Bank, I wondered what would be worse, turning out in the annual Jeparit grudge match, or ending up in a wrestling bout with Mario and some Moonee Ponds prostitutes? The nightmare scenario was that I could end up doing both.

Chapter 5:
Oxygen

I stagger down the corridor, the heat is killing. I'm having another of my Vincent van Gogh days. Earlier in the car park I was almost blinded by the dazzle from the chrome bumpers. Chrome blue, Prussian blue, wheat fields, crows in the sky. My ear begins to itch so much, I think I might just cut it off.

With a desperate lunge I make it into the science lab, where year 10 are waiting patiently. As I slide open the door, the air-conditioned coolness strikes me. It is delicious, like diving into a cold lake on the hottest day of the year.

The children are wonderful. Young adults, but different from city kids. For a start, they are both very polite and quite shy. They also have an interest in all things in the wide world outside Rainbow. Before and after lessons they sidle up to me, usually in pairs, to talk about anything that takes their fancy. They smile, they are enthusiastic and they care for each other; in short, they are a delight. Perhaps because of this, as if by a miracle, I snap into teacher mode and feel immediately better.

"What are we doing today Tommo?" someone asks, "can we do a proper experiment?"

They like 'proper experiments', especially if there is an explosion or two, which, given my recent record, is quite likely.

I've just got started when Andrew comes in from next door.

Andrew has got the year 12 biology group in after lunch and is doing some complicated experiment with Canadian pondweed. He has been growing it for ever, a lush emerald green profusion housed in a huge glass tank. It is his pride and joy. I think that what he wants to do is to get his class to measure changes in the rate of photosynthesis caused by an increase in the supply of oxygen.

He outlines what is involved. What he needs is to bubble a reliable source of oxygen into the tank and he asks if I can help. This is a really bad idea.

"Sure," I say, despite the fact that, at that moment, I have no idea how to produce oxygen. My brain is still a bit fogged from another heavy duty night at the Eureka Hotel. Still, I've got a few books and can always read up on it.

Then I remember my 'O' level chemistry days.

"Just heat up a compound which has a large oxygen radical in it – something with the formula ending in O_3 or O_4 should do," and looking at the shelves I select a large jar labelled *Potassium Chlorate* $KClO_3$ and hand it to him.

"Heat this up. It's quite unstable and it will go like a bomb."

About a minute after Andrew has left the room, thoughts come to me. Potassium Chlorate – where have I heard of that before? Ah yes, weed killer, that's it, but there's something else nagging at me. I start thinking about the IRA. Why, I wonder, am I thinking about the IRA?

Meanwhile, my kids are getting on with their work and my brain is taking a short vacation.

A TV image comes to me of a deserted street, it's a British street. No one is moving, everything is quiet until BOOOM! bits of cars and other debris are flying everywhere.

"Shit." I must have said this aloud because Jamie Wagner on the front row sniggers.

I have a terrible sense of impending doom and rush next door.

Andrew has got about half a kilo of powder in a retort, leading from which is thick rubber tubing designed to collect gas in some delivery jars. In good health and safety mode he is wearing a pair of plastic goggles which I don't think will be quite enough to save him. His class is bunched around waiting for something spectacular to happen and, if they are anything like most kids, hoping for something to go spectacularly wrong.

"Stop!" I yell. Andrew is brandishing the Bunsen burner like a flame thrower. It is on full bore. I lunge forward and hit the gas tap, the flame dies and I feel a trickle of sweat run down my armpit. "I've had a better thought," I say. At that moment I don't know what the better thought is, but it must be an improvement on a simulated IRA attack. "Let's leave it for now, and I'll see you at lunch time."

By midday I have had a brainwave – something else from my school chemistry days. I know, I'll dig out the electrolysis equipment and bung a few thousand volts through a pneumatic trough full of water – that will do the trick; even an idiot knows that in theory it should produce hydrogen at one electrode and oxygen at the other.

Hurriedly, I assemble the equipment, wire it up, switch on the current and wait…. and wait and wait… Eventually, after what seems like an age, tiny bubbles appear at each electrode.

"Bollocks!" At this rate I'll be here all week, and the clock is ticking.

I have another brainwave, shove some acid into the water. Somewhere in the inner recesses of my reptilian brain I have a faint memory that this will speed things up.

I reach for some concentrated hydrochloric acid and suddenly there's action. At the electrodes, water begins bubbling like crazy and gas begins collecting above them. I decide to test some of it. There are two columns of gas, one above each electrode. Just to make sure that everything is OK I decide to do a quick test. I open one of the two taps, bleed off some of the gas and insert a glowing taper.

There is a nice satisfying explosion so I know I've got hydrogen, so the other gas must be oxygen. Satisfied, I switch off the power, the bubbling stops and I wheel the kit into the biology lab.

"Just plug it in and let her rip," I say, pleased with myself. "Hydrogen will come out here," I say, pointing to one electrode, "oxygen from here," and I point to the other. "Connect some tubing to the oxygen and bubble it in. Your pond weed will love it. Oh, another thing, you can teach the class a bit about the properties of hydrogen while you are about it," and I explain the simple test for the gas.

Feeling pleased with myself I return to the safety of the preparation room and turn my thoughts once more to how to get out of this place. I'm beginning to feel really trapped. I'm aware that a few folks are trying to fix me up with some extra curricular activity with the hairdresser from Hopetoun who, it is reputed, can do amazing things with the hairdryer and some industrial strength hair lacquer. Even worse though, it seems like every step I take is being observed by everyone in town.

I'm musing over escape possibilities when I become aware of an acrid smell seeping under the door. A few seconds later, Andrew comes bursting in with the unwelcome news that something has apparently gone wrong with his experiment. He drags me along to the classroom and there, in the aquarium tank instead of his beautifully coloured pondweed is a sorry mat of pale brown mush.

My eyes begin to sting and stream. Quickly I shut down the experiment before matters become critical. Once I've opened all the windows and doors, my mind is now free to consider what is happening. In an instant I realise what has gone wrong. When I added the hydrochloric acid and subjected it to a blast of current, sure enough it produced hydrogen, but instead of oxygen the apparatus began pumping out pure chlorine. Now, not only is chlorine toxic, it is also a very strong bleaching agent, accounting for both the death and discolouration of the pondweed.

Andrew looks crestfallen. Not only is his experiment a shambles, but his prized botanical specimen is beyond recall.

I have to think quickly. "Jesus, some idiot must've wrongly labelled the acid. They've obviously put hydrochloric acid in the sulphuric acid flask. Whoever it was, they should be shot. It's a good job I was on hand otherwise somebody could've been badly hurt."

Andrew gives me a sideways look. I'm not sure he believes me, but it is the best I can do.

Unaccountably, my mind is suddenly off on vacation again and I start thinking it's a pity that this isn't the history class, because I could have turned it into an experiential lesson on the effects of gas attacks during the Gallipoli campaign. I consider mentioning this to Andrew, but wisely think better of it.

Looking back, I can see that it was from this point onwards that my reputation as a chemistry teacher started to go into decline, a fact which made it even more imperative to get out of there as soon as possible.

How I finally made my escape is a strange and wonderful tale which involves Mario, the Shark, some Mullumbimby Madness, a kangaroo and a dog called Brutus, but as I left the smoking chaos of the chemistry lab that afternoon all of that lay in the future.

Chapter 6:
Godzone country

One of the sixth formers, a tall, dark haired girl named Annette, gave me a note from her family inviting me to their property a few miles out of town.

Ross had forewarned me. "You'll get heaps of free tucker, the parents are always inviting new teachers out to dinner."

I could see several reasons why they might do this. For a start, the new teachers were an oddity, something of interest in a place where not much happened. Secondly, they wanted to make the newcomers welcome and hopefully persuade them not to shoot through at the earliest opportunity. I happened to believe, however, that the main reason for this custom was simple, folks were just being kind. Nevertheless, I really didn't want to go. I knew that over dinner I might be asked lots of questions, personal questions about my long term plans; questions which I really didn't feel like answering. Had I been living elsewhere, I could have simply said that I was too busy, ignored things and hoped that I wouldn't see any of the family for a while, but here that was impossible. I was sure to see the mother or the father at the pub or in the bank, and this would be embarrassing. Besides, how would Annette feel? Everyone at school knew I had been invited, and to turn down the invitation would make life awkward for her as well. So, I figured, I had to bite the bullet and try to enjoy myself.

Annette's family, the Richters, lived on an enormous wheat farm that lay on land as flat as the proverbial tack. Her great grandfather had arrived in the area sometime in the very early 1900s, not long after the railway line from Jeparit had been completed. Most of the early settlers were of German descent, and there were still lots of families with surnames like Fischer, Schumann, Schulz, Kruger and Heinrich.

We pulled up in the dust outside a large farmhouse which was like something out of an Andrew Wyeth painting, large, weatherboarded and two storied, painted white with lace curtains in the windows. Inside it was dark and cool, the space made heavy by the presence of solid wooden furniture and dark framed mirrors. The centrepiece of the house was the dining room, dominated by a large mahogany table with precisely arranged place settings, above which was an ornate chandelier.

Peter, Annette's father, was looking much more spick and span than I had ever seen anyone in town. His dark hair was slicked back and neatly parted, and instead of wearing Blundstone work boots he was sporting a heavy looking pair of brown brogues.

"Come on mate, I'll show you around the place." He led the way followed by me, Annette and her two brothers. Margaret, his wife, offered an apology. "I'm just finishing off the veggies. I'll catch you in a while."

Occupying pride of place was the barn. To call it a barn perhaps gives the wrong impression. It looked like, indeed it was, a very large steel shed about half the size of a football field, housing farming machinery that was industrial in scale. There were at least three enormous John Deere tractors, and a combine harvester that was as big as a small house.

After the kids had wandered off we got to talking.

"How are things going?" I asked.

"Tough, real tough. We only had four inches of rain last year, and if things don't improve, lots of us cockies will go under." Cockies? This was a new word for me, and Peter must have seen my puzzlement. "Cockies," he elaborated. "The gum trees round here are full of cockatoos, so for some reason they call the farmers cockies."

I knew how much the land was worth - despite the drought, about two million, I reckoned, and on top of that there was about half a million bucks' worth of gear, so I asked the obvious question. "Why don't you just sell up and go the city? For that sort of money you could buy a big place in Carlton and put your feet up."

Peter shot me a pitying glance. "This is our land, my family's and my kids', and it's the land of their kids as well. The only way you'll get me out of here is in a box." This connection with the land was strong, and it was real. The land that his ancestors had taken seemed to me like it was part of his family, and yet, in the current climate it seemed that the land and the cockies were entwined in a macabre dance that could have fatal consequences. If the drought did not break, then lives and dreams were going to be destroyed. Peter must have been reading my thoughts. "You heard about what happened at the Wagner place?"

I had. Just before I had arrived in town there had been an 'accident' with a shotgun and Stefan Wagner had lost his life. Hopefully his insurance policy would pay out, but questions were being asked. After all, it wasn't the first such accident in the area in recent times.

Peter was quiet. He silently stared across the empty paddocks of dried grasses, while in the distance a mob of sulphur crested cockatoos danced in the boughs of a stand of gently swaying eucalypts. "Doesn't do to think about things too much. The rain will come again and we'll be right." There was a long pause before he continued, "Time for dinner don't you think?"

I did think it was time for dinner, but I also thought that it might be time for people like Peter and his family to maybe think of other ways of earning a living. The drought had already been going for over a year and, for all anyone knew, it could continue for an age. In Europe, when we talk about climate we talk about minor variations from year to year, but here in the Mallee you could get twenty inches of rain one year, then almost none for two or three years. Farming here was like a game of Russian roulette with a gun that pointed at everyone's head.

Margaret came out and I thought she was going to call us in, but she just stood there with us, drinking in the beauty of the day's end. As we watched, the sun slowly began to sink, painting the sky the colour of blood and staining the haematite rich earth a darker red. "Beautiful, just beautiful. Now you know Tommo," she said, "why we call it Godzone country."

Yeah, it was Godzone country, and I wondered how long God would continue to lease it out the Richters, and I more than half reckoned that they were thinking pretty much the same thing.

Chapter 7:
What is your flesh?

A dark, blood-black stain is spread across the carpet. I lie staring at it for a while before I figure out what it is. It's my sleeping bag, which must somehow have ended up on the floor when I crawled in from my latest feat of horse racing prognostication at the Eureka Hotel.

Despite the heat, I shiver. My mouth feels dry, so I get up and walk into the kitchen to pull myself a glass of water. I drink it quickly and chase the dust from my throat. I pour another and wander back into the bedroom, glass in hand, and am about to get back into bed when I think I hear something in the backyard. I tense, pad to the window and cautiously pull the curtains aside to look.

There, sitting on the grass, are about fifty people, Aboriginals. I can see them quite clearly. They are eating, laughing and shouting, but I can't hear them. Between me and them is a blazing fire, sparks shooting up to the heavens and merging with a sky ink-black, yet full of stars.

I stare. Who are these people? What are they doing here? Am I dreaming? I close my eyes, will myself awake, shake my head, and reopen them. The scene is still the same.

It's incongruous. Here I am in the back of my bungalow watching what seems like a corroboree. It is strange, something is wrong; very, very wrong.

I look along the line of men. There are no women and no young children. I am aware that, although I can see them, they can't see me. It is as though I am observing from afar.

I watch for the longest time. I notice how they relate to each other and become engrossed in the ritual, and gradually I begin to relax.

As I feel more at ease, I get the odd feeling that my visitors are both there and not there, if you know what I mean. It seems to me that I am witnessing an event that has been played out before in this space, but a long time ago.

I begin thinking about the dreamtime in which Aboriginal people believe the past, the present and the future coexist. I feel instinctively that I am standing on a bridge that spans time and space and that the bridge is so incredibly beautiful and fragile that, if I make a false move, it could be destroyed. I also know instinctively that, if I choose to, I could transfer myself to the group simply by willing it, and this gives me a feeling of deep peace and contentment.

As I watch, my eyes fix on one particular young man, aged about twenty I guess, younger than most of the gathering. His skin shines in the firelight. He is laughing with his neighbours, pushing them and being pushed in return as they sit cross legged on the ground. His eyes are like jet and, as I stare into them, his story begins to unfold. I see his memories, the people he loves, the things that please him. He is fishing in the river, hauling yabbies and clams, pulling kumpung, the succulent bulrushes that form a staple of his diet, feasting on water lilies and dandelion yams and observing the changes in the heavens as the seasons come and go. On this night beneath the stars there is nothing within him to cause concern. Everything is as it should be. He feels deeply happy and his mood washes over me as I relax and yearn to join him.

Gradually, almost imperceptibly, I become aware that he feels he is being observed. His laughing and joking cease, his face becomes more serious, his eyes narrow and his thoughts are lost to me as he turns his head from side to side slowly, as if looking for something or someone.

I knew it was going to happen but there was nothing I could do about it. As he searches, he scans the area that I'm standing in. His eyes continue their tracking, moving past me for just a moment, then they flick back. His eyes lock on to mine. He can see me, I think; and realise that he is thinking the same thing.

We stare at each other. Time stands still. He can now see inside my mind and, unlike his idyllic images of hunting and collecting, I know that he is now seeing my life, one that is very alien to him. He is searching, wondering who I am and where I come from, trying to understand what he is seeing and how it fits into his conception of the world. I then become aware of something else, I feel distinctly that he is trying to ask me something, something very important, something that it is necessary for him to know.

The question forms in my mind.

"What is your flesh?"

The fire sparks, a log falls and he involuntarily looks away and, in that moment, the whole scene in front of me changes.

The backyard is empty. I am very confused and think that maybe I've been sleepwalking and have dreamt everything. Just to make sure though, I decide to look in the back garden to see if there is anyone out there. I slip the door lock and, with a degree of unease, step out. There's nothing, apart from a few blades of dried grass and the ancient Hills Hoist standing over to one side.

As I wander around, something very sharp penetrates the sole of my foot and I swear with pain, it is a bindi eye, about half an inch long and triangular in shape. One of its sharp, woody spikes has embedded itself deeply, and I limp indoors to remove it. I hop to my bed, sit down and swear again as I pull it out.

I put on my running shoes and go out for another look. I don't put on the outside light because, somehow, it feels sacrilegious.

Rainbow is dark and quiet; the only illumination is from the canopy of stars. I sit on the back step and reflect on what I've just experienced. I smile and close my eyes.

I woke sometime later. The sky was beginning to bleed the first light of day, and it was cold. I shivered, had a last look around, went indoors and dropped into bed. I lay back, thoughts swirling around my head, but nonetheless I think I must have been asleep again within seconds.

I was reawoken from a deep sleep by a loud banging at the door. I rolled over and waited for my visitor to leave. Another knock and then, a voice, "Tommo, shift yourself, it's nine o'clock." It was Mario. He had recently bought a new four wheel drive and announced that he was taking it for a spin to try it out. "Wanna come?"

"Sure, why not?" I mumbled. "Hold on a sec, I'll get ready."

As I showered, I thought about the night before and the dream that I'd had. It was still vivid. I finished getting dressed and noticed something on my bedside table. It was the bindi eye.

I looked at the sole of my foot and, sure enough, there was a matching puncture wound.

I grabbed some fruit, veggies, tahini and pitta bread together with a couple of beers, and dropped them into my eskie. I stuffed a couple of bars of chocolate in as an afterthought, and finally stowed my factor 50.

Mario was proud of his new Subaru. He walked around it proprietorially, pointing out various features, a bull bar, a winch, a water bag and large, wide sand tires.

We headed out north west and, around mid-morning, parked up at an abandoned homestead, a victim, no doubt of the droughts of the nineteen thirties and forties. The exterior was pretty much intact, but the doors and windows and parts of the roof were long gone. The yard was a mess of twisted corrugated iron wreckage assembled around the foot of an old Southern Cross wind powered water pump, its reinforced tower listing to one side and its slatted fan wheel and rudder-like tail twisted and bent. The bore water had clearly given out some time ago, as had the farm.

Dust hung in the heat as we fossicked around. We were about to leave when Mario thought he heard something.

"Listen." I heard nothing. "Listen." Yes, there it was, a scrabbling sound. Mario started to move. "It's coming from over there."

We came to a large well and looked down into it. It was about fifteen feet deep and bone dry, and the bottom was littered with broken bottles, cigarette packets and rusted tin cans. Amongst this debris was a large lizard. It was thrashing around, but couldn't seem to climb out. We couldn't imagine how it was stuck, but clearly it couldn't escape by itself. Mario found a large piece of wood and lowered it down and, by leaning it against one side of the well, we made a ramp down which I scrambled.

The lizard was large, and I was afraid he might bite, but he didn't. I saw the problem straight away, the creature had entangled a rear leg in some chicken wire. All I had to do was unravel the wire, and the lizard was free. For a moment it lay there blinking at me, and then it leapt onto the wall of the well and raced up to freedom.

Heading north, we soon entered the National Park that surrounds Lake Albacutya. We spent the rest of the morning exploring the local flora and tearing up and down the dry lakebed. The four wheel drive performed really well and the harder we drove it, the happier Mario became.

Sometime after noon we decided it was time for a bit of tucker. Mario picked out a likely spot, deep shade under some large gum trees at the edge of what, in wetter times, would be the lake shore. As we headed towards it, something on the far side of the lakebed caught my eye, a series of hummocks that were quite unlike anything else I'd seen that day. They excited my interest as an amateur geologist.

"Let's go and check those out," I said.

When we got there we found six or seven large mounds clustered closely together. Mario looked at me. "What do you reckon made these?"

"Dunno."

I began poking at one of the mounds with a stick. Immediately I unearthed shells, lots of them, perhaps thousands.

Mario got really excited. "Fish bones. Here's a couple of teeth, maybe from a 'roo."

In a couple of spots we found remains of charcoal, amongst which were charred fragments of ochre stained bone.

I realised what we had discovered. It was a corroboree site, and I'm guessing from its size that it was used for a long time; people would have come here regularly, over thousands of years maybe.

Neither of us had ever come across a corroboree midden before, so we were careful not to disturb things too much, but in all honesty, we could hardly have scratched the surface.

It was then that I saw him, walking across the lake bed. His gait was strange and slow, almost as though he were wading through shallows, A young man, alert, skin glistening in the heat, looking right and left; searching for someone, something. He looked towards me, and as he did he squinted and shaded his eyes from the sun as if he was having difficulty seeing. Our eyes locked and I felt the echo of his question: "What is your flesh?"

A breeze picked up from nowhere and a dust devil skittered towards me. Involuntarily I closed my eyes for a moment, and in that instant both the dust devil and the visitor were gone.

Mario was very quiet. "Did you see that?" I asked.

"Time to go," he said and pointed upwards. The sky was turning dark and the leaves on the gums were shuffling in a breeze that had suddenly sprung up. "If it rains, we could get stuck."

I thought this unlikely, but was aware that something had spooked him.

There was a far off rumble, and in the distance I could see dark cumulus clouds gathering in height. It was raining somewhere around Jeparit. The cockies would be celebrating in the Hindmarsh Hotel tonight.

The air was warm and sticky and the rumbles of thunder continued for some time. We drove back towards home and hardly spoke a word.

Chapter 8:
Stella

When we got back into town I decided to do a bit of research, and phoned the Wimmera mobile library based in Dimboola. The library visited Rainbow every couple of weeks and offered a limited range of literature, mainly pulp novels and advice on the use of superphosphate fertiliser. The folks who ran it gave me the impression that they had a lot of down time and were delighted to help anyone with any request, no matter how unusual. So, when I asked for books or articles on pre-European settlement of the region, they were only too happy to oblige.

A couple of weeks later I found myself keeping an appointment with a large converted bus parked outside the Eureka Hotel. Even from a hundred yards away I could see that business was slow; the street was deserted and it was so quiet that I could hear the metal frames of the grain silos grating as they expanded in the heat over half a mile away on the edge of town.

As I stepped in from the street I was met by the wonderful air-conditioned coolness of the interior. It took my eyes a few seconds to accustom themselves to the gloom within. There was no one at home, but there was a pile of books and papers with my name on it, along with a note: 'if you need any help you'll find me in the pub. I've left some articles for you on the desk'.

Sure enough there was an envelope, and inside was a swag of photocopied sheets. As I sat down to read, one caught my eye, it was a government publication entitled *Aboriginal Burials*.

What attracted me was a photograph on the front page. The image looked familiar, rather like the mound I had encountered at

Lake Albacutya.

As I read, I discovered some intriguing information.

Burials tend to be in soft soils and sand, although some burials also occur in rock shelters and caves. Soil or sand around the bones may be stained with charcoal or ochre. Shell, animal bone and stone tools may sometimes be present. They tend to be near water courses, or in dunes surrounding old lake beds. Many burials have been found on high points, such as dune ridges, within surrounding flat plains. They are often near or within Aboriginal occupation places such as oven mounds or shell middens.

As I was digesting this, someone else entered.

"G'day, you'll be Tommo I reckon. Have you had your bloods taken yet? I can do it at your place this arvo – it'll save you a trip to Jeparit."

I added up the zeros and realised that this must be Stella, the bush nurse I'd avoided ever since arriving in town on account of her fearsome reputation for trying to inject anything that moved. She was about 25 years old with tight curly hair and a smile as wide as the Mallee. Stella also had a reputation for dress sense. Despite the heat on the main drag she was wearing an ancient green woollen pullover that looked as though it had been chewed over by a pack of dingoes, and a baggy pair of Levis that had been washed the last time Lake Albacutya had water in it. The pièce de résistance, however, was an enormous pair of size twelve Wellington boots.

"Expecting rain are you?" I asked.

She smiled, showing a set of teeth that could have been designed by a Hollywood dentist. She sniffed the air, "A Pommie eh? How long have you been here?"

I laughed, I liked Stella. "Okay, enough of the personal hygiene jokes."

She grinned "Well lay off me wellies then, and maybe I'll forget about the blood tests."

I could tell straight away that Stella and I would get on like a house on fire. She was solid, in a good way, reliable; and I got the impression that she was the sort of person that, in a pinch, you could trust with your life.

Chapter 9:
Pure gold

I was in dire need of some wheels. Although there was nowhere really to go in Rainbow, I felt the need to be able to leave should the urge arise. The problem was that finding a good second hand car out in the Mallee was like looking for a needle in a haystack. The opportunity came when I had to go to Melbourne for an Education Department medical on the last Friday of the month. I made up my mind that, whatever happened, I wasn't going to come back without a car.

I saw it advertised in Thursday's copy of The Age. It was short and to the point:

1970 Chrysler Valliant Regal. V8, 318 cu ins. Twin Holly carbs. TorqueFlite auto. 80,300 RWC. $1350 ONO.

I called the number and a guy called Jeff answered.

"Hi, my name's Tommo, I'm phoning about the car," I said. "Is it in good condition?"

"She's a real beaut mate, runs like a dream, pure gold." He told me the car was at his place in Fern Tree Gully, in the Dandenong hills above Melbourne.

"When can I see it?"

"Anytime, – I've got two people coming round on Saturday but."

"How about tomorrow night, say six o'clock?"

"Sure, see you then."

I left him a contact number in Melbourne just in case the car was sold in the meantime, and continued looking through the used car ads. I was really after a VW because I knew them pretty well and they were usually reliable, but my priority was to get anything that was halfway decent for under fifteen hundred dollars.

As a new teacher, Andrew also had a medical lined up, so we planned to go together. Stella was coming along, as she said, to do some first aid training on dealing with fractures at a health clinic in town.

We left straight after school, around three on Thursday afternoon, and drove out through Birchip towards Wycheproof and beyond.

I must admit that Birchip made little impression. I understand that in recent years it achieved lasting fame as the two time winner of The Great Australian Vanilla Slice competition which, incidentally, was something that Jeff Kennett, the former Premier of Victoria, thought was of enormous importance, once declaring, "The pursuit of the best vanilla slice baker in Australia should be of great national interest. I encourage bakers throughout Australia to rise up and pit their skills against their peers..." Jeff Kennett, incidentally, inspired bumper stickers including 'I've had a Kennett of a day' and 'I feel absolutely Jeffed'. When we passed through Birchip all this was in the future, however, as the town sizzled in the late afternoon sun.

At Wycheproof Stella pointed out the local 'mountain', a pimple-shaped mound about a hundred feet high. We were still talking about this when we were almost totalled by a train running down the town's main street. This came as a bit of a surprise to me, but Stella and Andrew had apparently seen it all before.

As the sun went down a few kangaroos began bouncing across the road ahead and, while the sky turned from pink to crimson, the trees thickened with mobs of galahs.

At Wedderburn we pulled over and, as Stella and Andrew went off to take a leak, I went to buy us all coffee. I was served by a young woman who asked, "Are you's a fossicker?"

"Pardon?" The word sounded a bit, you know, rude.

She smiled. "We get lots of Poms around here. All looking for the same thing, if you get my drift." She looked at me in a way that I think was meant to tell me that she knew that I knew what she was talking about. I smiled back weakly, unsure where this conversation was going. "Would you like to see my nugget?" This is not a question I'd ever been asked. "If you come round the back I'll show it to you." She dumped the coffees on the counter, grabbed me by the arm and pulled me into a back room, closing the door behind her. "We don't want to be disturbed, now, do we?" On the contrary, at that moment I was very keen to be disturbed, especially when she said, in a throaty voice, "I think you'll like this." She pressed something into my hand: a glass jar containing a walnut sized object, gold in colour. "That's it. Whaddya think? Sure, it's not the Hand of Faith, but it's got to be worth a bit." I emptied the jar and rolled the piece of gold in my palm. It was heavy and warm to the touch, and when I dug my nails in they left a slight impression. "Ya can have it for a hundred bucks. I'll throw the coffees in for free."

And that's how I ended up owning my own little bit of Australia's goldfield heritage.

When I emerged Andrew and Stella were finishing their drinks, so we headed out to the car pretty much straight away.

"You didn't buy anything back there did you?" Stella asked.

"What do you mean?"

"A gold nugget perhaps?" And they both laughed.

Andrew went on, "A couple of years back some bloke with a metal detector found a huge nugget not far from here – weighed about thirty kilos. They called it the Hand of Faith. The story goes that about two weeks before the bloke had a dream about it and told his mates, and even drew a picture of it. Ever since then the locals have cottoned on and try to sell fake nuggets to unsuspecting tourists. Usually it's a small lump of lead decorated with gold paint."

I decided to keep quiet and to get rid of my purchase at the earliest opportunity, and probably would have done so had I not fallen asleep just a few miles along the road.

We were through the centre of Melbourne and entering Florence Street when I awoke. Trev's house was in darkness, even though it was only about 8pm. This didn't surprise me because Trev and Steph had World War II quality blackout curtains and, even at midday in the height of summer, very few photons ever penetrated the building.

Trev was horizontal on the living room settee wearing an enormous pair of headphones from which I could distinctly hear themes from Frank Zappa's epic work *Weasels Ripped my Flesh*.

I cracked a couple of tinnies, handed one to Trev and confirmed the details for the next day. I'd get the train into town and Trev would meet me after my medical and drive me up to Fern Tree Gully to see about the car.

By the time I'd finished the beer I was feeling pretty bushed, so I left Trev and Frank to it and sidled off to bed.

The following afternoon as I left the medical centre, I saw Trev's ute pull up to the kerb on Collins Street in a no standing zone.

"Get in mate before the parkies see me."

I jumped in and we headed out over the Swanston Street Bridge and drove east.

Fern Tree Gully lies in the foothills of the Dandenong Ranges about twenty miles from the city. As we snaked up the winding road that led from the freeway, the air was thick with the scent of eucalyptus and the metallic calls of bell birds.

Finding the car wasn't difficult. It was parked on the gravel along a straight stretch of road at the far end of town. Jeff was leaning against the bonnet and waved to us as we pulled in.

When I say I was shocked by the appearance of the car, that would be an understatement. It was a thing of beauty, all chrome and leather, with an engine that I reckon could take a payload to the moon.

I was invited to take it for a ride, so I levered myself into the driver's bucket seat and turned the ignition. The engine gave a powerful animal growl and at a touch of the gas, leapt forward.

Now, I know nothing about cars, but I could tell for sure that this was nothing like the VW Beetle that I hoped to buy. Not only was it about three times as long, but the speedo went up to 180 miles per hour. I could also tell it was the sort of car I could fall in love with.

When I got back, Jeff started banging on about things like the "five-litre V8", "the carbs" and the "torque", but I wasn't listening. I needed a car, and this looked perfect. I offered him $1200 and we quickly settled on $1250.

I remember driving back down to the main road behind Trev, thinking that I had got a pretty neat deal. I put on my sunglasses and felt as though I was becoming a character in a road movie.

We rolled up to the lights on the freeway. Trev was in the outside lane and I knew he would take off pretty quickly once the lights changed. Just as he did so, I put my foot to the floor. The wheels squealed and burnt rubber. The car leapt forward. In seconds I had hit 70 miles an hour. I nudged the gas and the speedo rocketed: 80, 90, then 100, and clearly there was much more to come. The buzz was immense and the ride was incredible, just like floating on air.

I remember easing the power back down and allowing Trev to catch up knowing that I had acquired a new and powerful friend. Something big, dark and dangerous. I christened it there and then: The Great Shark.

Little did I know that, before long, it was going to take me into troubled and unchartered waters.

Chapter 10:
The garden of earthly delights

I was making the most of not doing very much at Trev and Steph's house, indeed, I was enjoying things so much I decided I could afford to get up really early on Monday morning and floor it all the way back to Rainbow and roll straight into school.

At about tea time on the Sunday, however, I got a call from Mario. He'd heard that I had gone down to town and suggested meeting up.

"I'm around myself tonight, I'll be arriving in Moonee Ponds at around eleven. We can have a few beers, pick up the veggies at Vic market, you'll like that, and then head back home. Waddya think?"

Having slept for most of the weekend I wasn't fazed by the idea of a late night, besides, both Trev and Steph said that seeing the wholesale market in full swing would be an experience. In hindsight, they were not wrong.

Moonee Ponds is not everyone's cup of tea; in fact, I don't think it even partly resembles anyone's cup of tea. I remember, long afterwards, visiting a tourist office and reading a leaflet about the ten best things to do in Moonee Ponds. At the top of that list, someone had written a one word entry in black biro, 'leave'.

The address Mario had given me was for a bar, and I guess I should have known what to expect. I mean, if I had thought about it, the name, *Dazz's Romper Room* should have set the alarm bells ringing. It was the sort of place Trev liked to call a 'chew and spew', offering 'All You Can Eat for $5.50'.

The place was sandwiched neatly between a chip shop and a bookies, and looked as though the owners had recently been on a mission to collect all the garbage in town; the frontage was almost completely obscured by three dumpsters, behind one of which someone was bent double and looking for a mate called Huey.

Inside, the air was thick with a strange, smoky sweetness. Mario was holding a very large hand-rolled cigarette, a weighty number which he lit, tugged on heavily and passed to a woman on his left, Janice. Also at the table was a tall, dark haired woman. She told me that her name was Hilary. Janice smiled, took a toke and passed it on. I grabbed hold and took a long pull.

Almost immediately I begin to sense that I'm falling from a great height and close my eyes. When I open them I'm up there, among the stars, and I can see ....everything!

Things are beginning to happen surprisingly quickly. Mario has a smile as wide as Australia and is giving an amusing rendition of *Up There Cazaley*, and Janice looks as though she has been hit on the head by a blunt and very heavy object.

Meanwhile, I am transported through time and space. I'm out of there. I'm sitting with friends on a tropic beach, around a fire. The flames, fed by the sea salt on the blazing driftwood, burn crimson. Gum resin constantly pops as embers climb lazily into the air.

I feel it. I am beginning to fall. A jolt. I'm back at Trev's house, but now my clock is running backwards. It's as though I'm watching a movie of my life in reverse. Time is flying back until I'm in very familiar place. I'm at home in my cot and having a nightmare in which things are not what they seem. The movie runs forward, slowly, a day at a time, until, after what seems like years, I am back with Mario and Janice.

A volcano, which I had hitherto been unaware of, erupts in a rainbow coloured fountain from my head. This is not altogether unpleasant, and I'm surprised that no one has commented on it. I am also becoming aware that something is stirring in the recesses of my mind, something small and gentle like a tiny bird fluttering. Then, quite quickly, the fluttering increases in frequency and scale until I recognise it for what it really is, rising panic. I have been here before and, unless I am very much mistaken, I know what I am in for.

I find myself walking to the corner of the room, where I stand staring at the intersection of two walls. From somewhere, a long way away, I can hear Janice asking if I am all right, but I can't answer. In fact, all my muscles seem locked, and I have an awful feeling of certainty that I'm going to be trapped here, possibly forever, without being able to speak or move. Nowadays I know that they call this locked in syndrome, but at that moment all I know is that I am trapped and it is horrible.

I can still hear Mario singing away, and then the tone of his voice changes to one of concern. Something tells me that Janice isn't feeling too bright. Almost as soon as I have this thought, a tidal wave of fear courses through my body. I can see my watch, and the second hand appears to be almost stationary. I become aware that the only part of me which is capable of movement is my heart and, if my watch can be trusted, it is galloping like the clappers. I again try to move, but I still can't. I look at my watch face and count my pulse. It is fast, somewhere over 250 beats per minute, enough to kill a racehorse. With this thought, my heart puts on an extra spurt and my chest feels as though it is about to burst.

I know that I just have to relax, but how?

Just focus, I tell myself. I have clearly taken something that has speeded up part of my metabolism whilst locking up the rest. My priority is my heart which, unless I get it under control, is almost certainly going to give up on me.

In the background I am dimly aware that someone else has

entered the room. "It's Mullumbimby Madness mate," I hear him say.

Holy fucking baloney, that's all I need. Even in my sedated state I'm aware of what this stuff, the most psychotropic weed on the planet, can do. But things are about to get worse, a lot worse.

Through a maelstrom of sound I hear a conversation sounding to me as if it's coming from twenty thousand leagues under the sea.

"It's been dosed with horse tranquiliser."

"What?"

"Horse tranquiliser. Angel dust. Whatever you do, don't smoke any."

Thanks for the heads up, I think to myself. Now, I'm not sure how much of this stuff it takes to stop your average racehorse in its tracks, let alone the favourite in the three fifteen at Flemington, but in my condition I wouldn't even manage to stagger round the parade ring.

Next, I'm having what Trev would call an out of body experience. It's quite unpleasant. I can see Mario, Janice and Hilary dragging me outside and putting me in the car. My car. I see myself in the driving seat and can see Mario giving me instructions. I can't hear what he's saying but somehow I get the message. Mario wants me to drive. To follow him wherever he's going. Under normal circumstances this is the last thing I would have done in this condition, but I'm in what, in retrospect, I'll call zombie mode. In other words, if any one says do it, I'll do it.

With a herculean effort I look at my watch. Two thirty. I vaguely wonder where the last three hours have gone.

Then it's all engines running, and I'm at one with the Great Shark which, seems to have taken control. We are following some red tail lights which keep zooming in and out of focus. My head feels so heavy and I'm aware that somewhere in the car there's a vicious green snake that is just gagging to stick its fangs into me.

Sometime later we pull to a halt. It is as though I am in a Dutch medieval painting, a tumble drier of noise and light. As the scene swings in and out of focus I can see high sided trolleys being pushed past loaded with greenery. It's then that I think I realise where I am. I reckon I'm in Hieronymus Bosch's Garden of Earthly Delights. But I'm not. If only I could have raised my head a little I would have seen it, a large painted sign which says 'Welcome to Queen Victoria Market, the largest open air market in the Southern Hemisphere'.

Mario is clearly made of stern stuff. He hauls me out of the car. I'm not sure what language he is speaking as I can barely understand a word, but apparently a man with an unpronounceable name is going to load up Mario's wagon, and all I have to do is make sure it all gets aboard safely.

I sit on the loading bay and wait. I'm feeling edgy. From time to time a wave of fear courses through my body, and I feel a sense of impending doom. I just want to get out of this place as soon as possible.

It is then I see him, a burly, scar faced porter wheeling a huge trolley laden with zucchinis and other assorted vegetables. He is clearly searching for someone and, instinctively, I know he is looking for us. I see his name badge and call to him by name. I find that often helps when you're in a hurry.

"Franco, I think that's for us," I jab my thumb at the trolley. He looks puzzled. I reckon it's because I'm probably not speaking very clearly, so I grab him by the collar and yelled, "THAT – in THERE!" and point to Mario's truck.

He then says something I don't understand, "Scarabelli?"

I assume he is asking me in Italian if I am feeling OK – so I nod and, as I am still having difficulty stringing my words together and

I have no idea what, or who, Scarabelli is, I simply mutter, "Si." That does the trick.

Feeling quite pleased with myself I go to try and find Mario while the gear is being loaded. Fortunately, I don't need to go far. He is at a table drinking espresso and strega. He orders some for me and I take a big belt.

The result is electrifying, and my powers of speech immediately return. I explain that we are all loaded up and that I am keen to go as I am due to be teaching in less than five hours' time.

As we get up to leave I can see that Mario has something on his mind. He is quiet for a few moments then he speaks, slowly.

"What was in that stuff we smoked last night? Rainbow dust, right?"

"Angel dust."

"Same thing." He pauses. "Fucking Rainbow dust."

As we pull out of the loading bay I notice another truck, very similar to Mario's, being loaded alongside. Unfortunately, what I don't see is the name of the owner emblazoned on its side, *Scarabelli Brothers, Importers and Exporters.*

Chapter 11:
Blackjack

Things like this didn't happen on Scarabelli's patch. The consignment that had gone missing belonged to someone higher up the food chain, and that was a big worry. Whoever was responsible was going to end up having his subscription to Life magazine cancelled prematurely. The only lead he had was Franco.

Scarabelli sat on his swivel chair and methodically thumped the leather blackjack into his palm. Franco looked distinctly uncomfortable. The mix up at the loading bay was an easy mistake to make, but one which he knew was likely to have fatal consequences for someone. His shirt and trousers were soaked with sweat, and Scarabelli could smell the fear rising from his pores.

"I'm only gonna ask it this once. Who were the wise guys who drove off with our merchandise?"

Franco's face, which already had more stitches than a football casing, was a mask of pain. One of his eyes was closed, the other red with blood. He squirmed and his voice croaked, "There were two of them, they seemed to know what they were after. They told me to load the stuff and I did." The blackjack hit him again, this time across the mouth, exploding his bottom lip. Franco knew that his time on this earth was limited and, unless he gave Scarabelli something concrete, he was probably going to end up in concrete himself, and his final journey was probably going to be more painful than he could possibly imagine. Franco began to talk. "One guy I've seen here before. The other one was new to me. He seemed to be in charge and was giving the orders. He knew exactly what he was after and made me load the truck. He told me he was collecting it for you."

Scarabelli took his handgun from his coat pocket. It felt heavy and powerful. He admired its smooth lines and dull sheen. He smiled. Of all the things in the world this was probably the closest to his heart. He placed it on the table.

Franco was looking at the floor. He didn't want to look up, hoping against hope that somehow, some way, he might come out of this alive. Despite the pain, his mind was racing trying to think of anything that might save him.

There was something that he had seen in the bed of the truck as he loaded it. Something unusual. Something that, if he could only remember, might save his skin.

He heard a metallic click, a weapon being cocked. Then his mouth was forced open and he could taste the steel and oil of the gun barrel. It was cracking his teeth and bleeding his gums. His mind began spinning like a Catherine wheel on New Year's Eve and, as he waited for the bullet to smash through his head, he saw in his mind's eye the object he was trying to remember, a piece of newspaper lying in the back of the truck.

He could smell the nicotine on Scarabelli's hands and the stench of his own urine as he fought to speak. He could sense the trigger finger tightening and squeezing and then the hammer coming down. His mouth filled with blood. He tasted gunmetal but he was still alive. The gun was empty. Scarabelli was toying with him like a carnivore with its prey.

Franco was trying to speak but his tongue seemed to have a life of its own, so he raised his hand and began gesticulating wildly as Scarabelli decided to bring the interview to a finale and inserted a clip of ammunition.

Franco did the only thing he could think of. He hoped it would be enough. He started writing with his index finger using his own blood as ink. Two words appeared on the desk in front of him.

Jeparit Bugle.

Maybe it would be enough.

Chapter 12:
Diego Scarabelli's story

Scarabelli came from a good family, well connected. His father had once been a good friend of Francesco, 'The Toad', Tognoni. This was back in the 1950s, before the outbreak of the Market Wars, a vicious turf battle over control of Melbourne's Victoria Market.

He had started working the market in around 1960 with a schoolfriend, Lenny Landolpho, who for some reason no one could quite remember, had acquired the nickname 'Lucky'. They were smart boys, ambitious and quick on the uptake and so, one evening when they were asked to assist on an out of hours job, they agreed. It involved a cement contract for the Westgate Bridge, which was being built at the time. The boys had no idea when they set out that night that their world was about to change forever.

The meeting was held in a warehouse just outside Essendon, close to the old airfield. Scarabelli and Lenny arrived early. Their job, they were told, was to keep a look out for unwanted visitors.

Shortly after sundown, people began to arrive. Scarabelli only recognised one: a menacing, thick set man who had a well deserved reputation for violence: 'Sunshine Sam' Gioconda.

Eight men went into the meeting but only seven left. Diego and Lenny were given the task of tidying things up afterwards. It wasn't pleasant, but Diego learnt several things:

Firstly, if anyone wanted an argument and they wouldn't see sense, there was only one way to end it.

Secondly, decisive action impressed friends and enemies alike.

Thirdly, if you ever made a mistake you had to clear it up yourself before anyone else did.

Fourthly, that Sam Gioconda never gave anyone a second chance. The Gioconda family could not afford to let anyone, no matter how big or small, get away with anything. The loss of some of Sunshine Sam's merchandise from the back of one of his capo's trucks was, as they say, 'un insulto', and could not be tolerated. Someone would have to pay for this and, unless he acted quickly, that someone would be Scarabelli.

Scarabelli called in a few friends and began to plan a recovery operation. He had to act fast. The one lead he had was the newspaper. He'd be heading out to Jeparit in the morning, but first he'd have to find out where it was. In the meantime, he had to finish that business with Franco.

Chapter 13:
A Ton of super

At lunch time, back in the staff room there was a pile of messages. All from Mario.

The messages were simple, "I need to talk to you as soon as possible." I assumed that he needed an alibi for Allegra and I began wondering what transgressions had taken place while I had been indisposed at Moonee Ponds.

I drank a glass of water and walked down the corridor out into the blazing afternoon sun.

Allegra was serving when I walked into the shop. She was a tall, rounded woman of about thirty-five, dark and beautiful with a charming smile – charming, until that is, she saw me.

"What the fuck happen with Mario? He not himself today." I raised my hands in self defence and stepped back as she marched towards me. "You been with him at that Rompy Room with them women?"

This reference to Dazza's place came as a bit of a surprise.

I was spluttering an answer when Mario entered from the main street. He was sweating and seemed agitated. He grabbed my arm and dragged me out to the rear of the store.

Under the shade of the back veranda Mario started talking. Fast. So fast that I couldn't get the gist.

"Slow down mate, I can't understand what you're saying."

He motioned me towards the cold store. "Take a look in there." As he opened the door, the fluorescent light kicked in. I looked, but wasn't sure what I was supposed to see.

"What?" I asked.

"There," – and Mario jerked his thumb at a large pile of fertiliser sacks. There must have been about fifty, all labelled 'SSP, Single Super Phosphate, 25 Kg'. I was still at a loss.

I began thinking about parallels with Stan's braces, and how long it would take to sell this lot. "You seem to have a shed load. No pun intended. Where did you get it all?"

Mario gave me an odd look. "Where did *I* get it? I left you with the wagon last night and you loaded it right?"

"Sort of, yeah."

"Well, when I looked this morning, I'm missing half the veggies and I've got a ton of this shit."

I wasn't sure what was going on, or why I was suddenly responsible. We were both quiet for a moment before I saw a glimmer of hope that there might, after all, be an upside to this mix up. "Look, the cockies will take it off your hands – they're always banging on about worming tablets and the price of 'Super'. You'll have no problems."

"Thanks, that's reassuring mate. The only problem is, this stuff is a bit more super than you think." Mario thrust his hands into an incision he'd made into the side of one of the sacks and pulled out a pile of very strong smelling green stuff. The odour and appearance was unmistakable. "Mildura's finest."

This certainly wasn't something I'd seen coming and, looking at Mario's expression, it was clearly something that had not featured strongly in his Jeparit Bugle horoscope.

The question now was, what to do with it?

Mario wanted to know exactly how all of this gear had ended up in his van and I tried to help as much as I could – which wasn't a lot.

"Look, I was in a bit of a state. I remember a bloke with a pallet. I think he said he was looking for you. He seemed quite a nice bloke once I managed to see past the scars."

Mario winced. "Did he say anything?"

"Yeah, I think so."

"Go on."

"I think he asked if I was all right. He was speaking Italian."

Mario looked worried, "That figures." He was quiet for a few moments then he spoke, slowly. "We've got to keep quiet about this. It belongs to some important people. We've been lucky so far so let's just lie doggo and hope that no one comes looking."

And that's how we should have left it, but Mario, being Mario, couldn't keep as quiet about it as he should have. A couple of days later a mysterious supply of dope materialised at a lock-in at the Jeparit pub, and then a couple of days after that I saw a stranger in a suit engaged in deep conversation with Mario on Federal Street. Instinctively, I knew at that moment that Rainbow's second worst kept secret was out of the bag, both literally and metaphorically, and it would only be a matter of time before some rather unpleasant people came sniffing around. Before they did, I had to have a meeting to clear the air with Mario. I can now see that it was almost already too late.

Chapter 14:
The silos

I wake to the sound of my alarm.

Early mornings in Rainbow are like nowhere else on earth. It's quiet, not a sound. There's just silence. Sometimes, on days like this, I feel that if I listen carefully I might even be able to hear the earth spinning on its axis.

As I step out on to the back porch, the air is still and as cool as fresh spring water. The sky is dark velvet with streaks of crimson along the rim of the world. It is the best time of day. A time without time, a time to be out running in the great wide openness that lies beyond the doorstep.

I take my key from the hook by the door and lock up. I'm not sure why I do this, habit I guess. In Rainbow no one ever locks their homes, but I do it anyway, and put the key in my shorts pocket.

I start at a gentle pace to warm up and lope to the main road, taking a left down past Bill's caravan, which, for once is quiet. His dogs are still slumbering as the sky begins to redden. I take another left along a dirt track that separates two enormous fields, paddocks as they are known locally. Each one is a mile square so I know that my loop is four miles and I will run it in twenty-eight minutes. Today, however, if I'm feeling good, I might go a mile or so further.

As I run, I'm aware of the sound of my feet on the gravel and my breathing, laboured at first but gradually settling into a steady rhythm. Within five minutes I am transported. I'm profoundly relaxed and my mind goes wherever it wants to go. There is no effort needed. Distance just flows beneath my feet.

At the first turning the sun breaks through a pencil line of cloud and illuminates baubles of dew which glitter like diamonds in the grass and, for the next few minutes, I run along flanked on either side by colourful displays of nature at its finest.

In the scrub that makes up the paddock boundaries the tangled fishing net of a web belonging to a Mallee spider is glittering in the frost, lying in wait for the sun and any unsuspecting insects.

At the next turn there's a rustle in the undergrowth, and a couple of redthroats fly up almost into my face. They are small with a bright flash on their breast; when I first arrived in Rainbow I thought they were robins, but apparently they belong to an entirely different species.

It is still cool, but the temperature is rising with every step I take. The moon is high and the sky is now a dark blue. I smile to myself and think that I don't need to tune into the weather forecast to tell that the day is going to be a hot one.

I'm heading back towards town, and by the time I hit the Birchip road I'm feeling good, so I decide to extend my run by taking a trail that leads to the grain silos and then back home via the stockyards.

The silos are about two hundred feet tall and made of grey concrete. In the flatlands of the Mallee they can be seen for miles. They were once the beating heart of the town but now they are abandoned, the offices caked in dust and rubble, with metal girders piled up around the back. There's no one around so I stop my watch and decide to explore. I clamber over some decaying wooden pallets to peer in at a window. Through the grime I can see what was once an office, desks and chairs still in place, while on the shelves heavy ledgers sit, awaiting the visit of an auditor who will never come.

After a brief pause I scramble back and, as I do, I slip and cut my knee on an old spar. The wound isn't deep, but it is bleeding surprisingly heavily. I take off my running vest to apply pressure, and it soon stops. I brush the dirt from my palms where I've broken my fall, restart my watch and continue my run.

By the time I get to the stockyards my leg is bleeding again and now it's beginning to hurt – especially when I clamber over the wooden fencing that runs alongside the main road.

The tarmac is warm beneath my feet and already the air is much warmer than it was half an hour ago. I hear birdsong, and startle a mob of regent parrots who take to the air in a kaleidoscope of colour.

In a couple of minutes I'm back at my door. I stop my watch and check the time. I've been out for thirty-seven minutes, so I know I've covered just over five miles. It's still not yet seven o'clock, but it feels that already I've lived the whole day and more. And there's a problem, somewhere on the run I've managed to lose my door key, probably when I fell back at the silos. Fortunately, I know that Ross keeps a spare in the outhouse, and in a couple of minutes I'm indoors drinking filter coffee.

As I warm down, I examine my leg. Everything is fine. Although there's been plenty of blood it's no big deal, and there's no need for stitching. I check the time and realise that I need to get a shift on or I'll be late for school. I take a quick shower and get dressed. I mean to chuck my running gear into the laundry basket but, as is my habit, I leave it for the time being on the bedroom floor along with some other unwashed clothes, grab my books and set off for work.

I didn't know it then, but that bloodstained vest was going to send quite a few people on a wild goose chase over the next few days and weeks.

Chapter 15:
Clearing the air

Later that day, I was just finishing teaching a chemistry class, and had narrowly avoided blowing up the sixth form again when the school secretary gave me a message.

"Something about health insurance," she said, handing me a slip of paper with a name and a phone number on it. I folded it up and put in my pocket. I had other things on my mind.

When I got home I was edgy. I felt hot and distinctly sticky, perhaps because I was worried; after all, Mario's shed was now probably the most valuable and dangerous piece of real estate in the Mallee, and its contents were weighing on my mind.

It wasn't only that, there was something else and I couldn't quite put my finger on it. I made a cuppa, sat on the back porch and began marking some school books. It was something that always took my mind off things, and sure enough it worked because in no time at all I fell fast asleep, and when I woke a couple of hours had passed.

The air was warm and damp and there was something not quite right. It took a while for me to figure it out and then it dawned on me. The sky was black. That's not so unusual, you might think, but in Rainbow the skies were never black, they were always full of stars.

I was pondering this when the phone rang. I padded inside, wondering who could be calling. When I picked up, I could hear Mario at the other end. He sounded as though he was about to have an asthma attack.

"Tommo, they are on to me."

"What? Who's on to you? What are you talking about?" Before he answered me though, I think I already knew, and I felt a wave of panic.

"The Italian mob, they'll be sniffing around soon if they aren't already. I might be paranoid, but about three times today I've seen a yellow Holden cruising the streets and it's given me a bad feeling." He was talking quickly. "I've sent Allegra to see her sister in Adelaide and told her to lie low." Mario was clearly worried about reprisals.

"Mario, just give the stuff back."

"I can't, I've already sold a big chunk of it." My fears were confirmed – of course that explained the guy in the suit. "Now listen Tommo, I've got a plan." In the sky lightening fizzed, illuminating a biblical collection of cumulonimbus clouds, and a few seconds later there followed a long, rolling boom.

The plan was cunning in its simplicity. So cunning that it could only have been designed by an idiot or a genius. As Mario elaborated, I felt I was having another out of body experience. The plan involved Stella, her bush clinic down the road at Jeparit, an industrial quantity of plaster of Paris and about half a kilometre of crepe bandages. "All you need to do, Tommo, is get out of town and leave the rest to me. You don't have much time. Get going. Now."

Mario sounded distressed, and his fear got to me. I pulled on some clothes, stuffed some gear into a bag and was about to go out to the car when I found the piece of paper scrunched up in my pocket.

I flattened it out and read the message:

Tommo, a Mr. Scarabelli called. He's at the Golden Nugget Motor Inn. Wants to talk about life insurance. Says it's urgent.

I grabbed the phone. I needed to tell Mario. He picked up straight away.

"Tommo leave, fast. Can't talk now. Just drive. Leave town. Get yourself to Jeparit. I'll be there outside the pub."

As I put the phone down there was another crash of lightning and the power went out all over town. I waited for the heavens to open and bring blessed relief to the parched earth, but it seemed as though the sky gods were having a joke. Instead of rain, a gust brought a whiplash of soil and grit that rattled the window pane.

The dust was swirling on Jeparit's main street as the Shark crawled towards the Hindmarsh Hotel. I cut the lights and the motor and rolled forward almost silently. Everywhere was as dark as a bag. The power was down here as well. Looking around I could make out what looked like a bottle shop and an op shop. As my eyes adjusted to the darkness, I noticed a grotesque figure in the gloom. It resembled an off colour abominable snowman. I squinted, and then realised I was looking at a fibreglass representation of what can only be described as a down and out koala which had suffered years of steroid abuse.

"Mario" I whispered, "Are you there?" There was no response, just the sound of the wind crashing through surrounding countryside. I waited and looked around carefully. Another flash of lightning lit up the sky. "It's Tommo," I whispered. "It's safe to come out. There's no one else here."

I'm not sure which I saw first, the leaflet taped to the koala's hand or the yellow Holden across the street with an 'Eat beef you bastards' bumper sticker.

Clearly Mr. Scarabelli was already here. Instinctively, I stepped back into the shadows, and not a moment too soon. As I caught my breath, a phone rang, right on the corner, not ten yards away. There was a muffled grunt and a cough and the Holden's door opened, the occupant heaved himself out and walked to the phone box. There then followed some animated discussion before the man put the receiver down, lit a cigarette, took a long and voluminous piss in the gutter, got back into the car, turned the ignition and drove off.

I waited a couple of minutes to check that the coast was clear. I was hurrying back to the car when I remembered the leaflet taped to the koala's hand. It might be nothing, but it could be a message.

Taped face up was a message addressed to 'Cazaley'. I grinned. I grabbed the piece of paper and unfolded it. It was in Mario's handwriting and simply said, "Leave."

Chapter 16:
Mr. Nicholson

After I got Mario's message I decided to look after my own health insurance, got into the Great Shark and headed out of town as fast as my wheels would take me. I had no real idea which way to go. I figured that my unwanted visitor would expect me to flee to Melbourne, so I headed in the opposite direction, back through Rainbow and north up the inland road towards New South Wales and eventually Queensland. I figured that if I put a few hundred miles between me and my Italian friend, I would be safe. The problem was that the Shark was rather conspicuous and, as I floored it along the outback roads, I was terrified that it might give me away.

Perhaps the worst bit was driving back through Rainbow. My nerves were jangling and I was constantly scanning for signs of any pursuers. I was too frightened to take the main road, so just before I reached town I took a left round the back of the stock yards and up to the grain silos before rejoining the highway.

As I drove north I kept an eye out, but after a couple of hours I began to feel a little more at ease and started to calm down a little.

I saw them as I crossed the Murray at Swan Hill, headlights in my rear view mirror, about a couple of miles behind. My stomach lurched and I told myself not to panic; after all, it could have been anyone. For the next hour I kept my foot down on the gas and eventually hit the Newell Highway just as the sky was beginning to lighten. I kept going as far as the small country town of Hay, where I decided to fill up. I was still on edge, so I didn't waste any time. It was just as well because, just as I was getting back into the Shark, I saw them again. Away back, on a long, straight stretch of road, a yellow blob was boiling up a plume of dust and racing towards me. I turned the ignition and roared back onto the highway. Now I knew for certain that I was being hunted down. Fortunately, I had two things going for me, a five-litre engine and an enormous petrol tank. I was sure I could outrun anyone.

I drove constantly through the dawn and the rest of that day, apart from a couple of hurried and nerve wracking petrol stops. I remember in particular pulling into a gas station at Narrabri and waiting for an age while the cashier fussed over giving me my exact change.

As I drove, I constantly checked the mirror for unwanted guests. A couple of times I saw vehicles behind me, but none of them ever got close enough for me to check them out. I carried on, driving fast, until, about twenty hours after I left Rainbow, exhaustion hit just outside Rockhampton. I was desperate for rest and looked for a place away from the main road. I found the perfect spot, on the back streets alongside a wide, sluggish river, the Jolly Swagman Camping and Caravan Park.

I was greeted by the owner, "G'day. How you goin'? I'm Frank."

I paused, something told me not to reveal my real name.

I shook his hand and gave him the first name that came to mind, "I'm Jack."

When I filled in the registration form I had to add my surname and, for some reason, I couldn't have been thinking clearly, I wrote 'Nicholson'.

Frank handed me a set of keys and a sticker for the car windscreen.

"What's this for?" I asked.

Frank smiled.

"We get a few folks sneaking in and trying to camp for free. This just helps us keep an eye on things".

I smiled and felt slightly reassured. I got back into the Shark, put the sticker on the windshield and made my way to my overnight van. That night I slept for twelve hours straight.

The next day, however, I had a nasty surprise when I came to check out and discovered that, in the rush to leave the last petrol stop, I had left my cheque book and bank card behind. After paying my bill I had only a few dollars left – not even enough for a tank of gas.

I was tired beyond belief, but pumped full of so much adrenaline that my mind raced through my options. It didn't take long because I really didn't have many. My only hope seemed to be to try to sell the Shark. It had to be worth a thousand bucks, and that could take me quite a way, quite fast.

Chapter 17:
Four down

I loaded up and drove into the town centre looking for a second hand car dealership. I was in a hurry to get away, and would have been in more of a hurry had I seen the yellow Holden which pulled into the Jolly Swagman car park about five minutes after I had left.

The traffic lights turned red as I pulled up at the bridge across the Fitzroy River; as I waited for them to change, I saw it. It was impossible not to. Painted bright pink and black, King's Cash Exchange was a pawn shop as big as a battleship, housed in what looked as though it had once been a classic Aussie pub. I drew up outside, realising that perhaps I didn't need to sell the car after all. Maybe I could sell something a little smaller, my camera perhaps? I grabbed the Olympus and wandered in.

As a teenager I had owned a pair of crepe soled brothel creepers, and the carpet in the pawn shop reminded me of them. The floor was spongy and rather sticky, as if designed to prevent anyone from making a quick getaway. Behind the counter sat a couple, or rather two versions of the same person. Between them they had a combined vocabulary, it seemed, of about fifty words, and they regarded me with almost total disinterest, if not contempt. The woman was smoking and filling in answers to a crossword. As I stood there, I found myself reading the clues.

Four down: Thick as...

"Shit," I said. I had meant this to be inaudible, but clearly it wasn't. The man looked up, offended. It was then I noticed a sign on the wall, *Foul language will not be tolerated*, above which was another,

Best prices paid for gold and silver. "I'll be back in a second." I needn't have said anything, because there was no answer.

I found it tucked away in the glove compartment, the glass jar with my sample of Wedderburn gold. I knew that it was probably worthless, but hey, it was worth a try. Back inside, I put it on the counter. "How much for this?"

The woman didn't even glance up. The man shifted his backside, and picked up the bottle, unscrewed the top and dropped the nugget into his palm. He then poked at it with a knife. Next, he produced a white tile and scraped the nugget across it. It left a yellow streak. Finally, he reached into a drawer and produced a small dropper from which he deposited a clear liquid onto the nugget. After a couple of moments, he wheezed, "Selling, or pawning?"

"Selling." His taciturn nature was infectious.

He produced a set of scales. I could see the weight, just under two ounces. "Five hundred bucks. Take it or leave it."

I was astonished. "What?"

"OK, five seventy-five. Last offer."

I nodded and waited as the cash was counted into my hands.

As I turned to leave, the woman spoke.

"Thieves," she said. I thought she was talking about her customers and didn't realise until sometime later that she had, against all the odds, actually solved four down.

After a nervous start, the day seemed to have taken a turn for the better. I had cash in my pocket, and still owned the car and my camera.

As I got back behind the wheel, I noticed the fuel gauge was flickering so I headed for the nearest garage and filled the tank up to the brim.

It was while waiting for my change that I saw it, the yellow

Holden cruising the main drag. It was about a hundred and fifty yards away when I eyeballed it, heading right towards me. I was a sitting duck but, just as I was about to leg it, a large van pulled in alongside and shielded the Shark from view. I held my breath as the Holden trundled past. I got back into the Shark, breathed slowly to calm myself, waited for a couple of moments, turned the ignition and rolled on to the main road, heading in the opposite direction to my pursuer.

Now, Australia is a big country and you'd think it would be easy to get lost. Well, maybe it is, but not necessarily so if someone thinks you might have a car boot full of Australia's finest and it belongs to them. I was still a bag of nerves.

Out of Rockhampton I drove inland and kept my foot down. From time to time I imagined I could see a vehicle in my rear mirror and was terrified of being caught. In the early evening I pulled off the road. Finding a spot which seemed well hidden, I tried to get a bit of rest, but it was impossible. My narrow escape had scared the bejesus out of me and I was wired. After half an hour or so, I fired the motor up again and drove through the night, fast. I was still going at a hell of a lick and feeling exhausted as dawn was breaking. Several times I found myself beginning to drop off, and for some reason kept seeing images of a strange guy with an axe screaming, "Here's Johnny!".

When I woke, the first thing I noticed was a kangaroo's head on my lap and my shirt soaked in blood. I felt like that guy in 'The Godfather' and waited for the pain to kick in.

Chapter 18:
The Wellshot Hotel

As I push the grinning head away from my chest I notice that the windscreen has been demolished. My mind stumbles back into gear and I begin to recall booming along an empty road and then being engulfed by an enormous explosion, my field of vision suddenly full of grey fur, claws and a grinning mouth. It slowly dawns on me that my car must have had a brief encounter with a rather large, now recently deceased, kangaroo.

Hitting a 'roo at eighty miles an hour is not recommended, either for cars or for kangaroos. The car is totalled and clearly the 'roo is no better off. So here I am, halfway across central Queensland in a pile of twisted metal and a heap of trouble. I now have no choice but to hump my lump on foot, all the time casting anxious glances over my shoulder.

A mile down the road I stagger into the wonderfully named Wellshot Hotel, a splendidly isolated place on the edge of nowhere. I lurch to a bar stool and order a nice frosty one to chase the dust, blood and kangaroo fur out of my mouth. I order a second one and begin to calm as the alcohol starts to neutralise the adrenaline that's pumping round my system. My eyesight seems a bit out of kilter and there is pain in my temple. I feel whacked and desperately tired but glad to be out of the sun, off the road and safe.

As my eyes begin to regain their focus, I begin to notice a few things.

For a start, at the bar is a fellow drinker. He has an ugly, weather beaten face. His hand reaches across to shake mine. A grip like iron, but cold as ice. His eyes are black and lifeless.

"Scarabelli," he says by way of introduction. "How about telling me a story Jack?"

Chapter 19:
Strange encounters of the third kind

Scarabelli stands and something nudges me in the ribs; it's hard, and I don't think it's a pencil.

"Get up, we're going for a little walk," he whispers.

I know exactly what is coming and I am not too keen on taking up the offer of a morning promenade.

As I rise from my stool, the door of the pub swings wide and a dazzling white light fills the entrance. I can vaguely make out two figures stepping in out of the heat, silhouetted by the glare. It reminds me of that scene from *Close Encounters of the Third Kind,* the one where the aliens introduce themselves.

A huge man steps into the darkened interior accompanied by a short, stocky woman whom I assume, correctly, is his partner.

"Two pots!" he yells at the barman even before he takes his seat, "and a couple for me new mates here," signalling to me and Scarabelli.

"Sorry mate, we're just leaving," says Scarabelli, but I've seen my chance.

I sit down immediately and say, with feeling, "Don't mind if I do."

I've only just got the glass to my lips when the barman asks the new arrival with almost indecent haste, "Having another, Norm?"

Norm nods, "Yeah and while you're at it, another for me Missus and me mates."

We make our introductions. Norm's wife is Brenda and she doesn't talk much, she just sits there drinking and studying the latest runners and riders at Flemington. Scarabelli is also quiet, and I know he's figuring just how to get me out of here. Just to keep things on the boil I order another round.

Scarabelli is getting distinctly agitated and stands up.

"Time to leave," he says, looking at me.

"BULLSHIT!" yells Norm. "Settle down, yer flaming mongrel, Jack and me have got some serious drinking to do."

Ten minutes later I'm rapidly entering a critical juncture. My bladder now contains about five pints of Castlemaine XXXX and I'm beginning to squirm. The problem is that if I go to the dunny, Scarabelli is likely to accompany me, and that will be the last time I risk spraying my running shoes.

To distract myself, I glance around the bar. The first people I see are two young blokes at a table to one side of us. The table has about an inch of stale beer on its surface and the two are lying face down in it. Dead to the world.

The only other person is a tall and dignified Aboriginal bloke standing immobile near the back door. He looks vaguely familiar. He's wearing a khaki shirt, tan shorts and heavy Blundstone boots. He holds a pot in his right hand and is staring into a horizon I cannot see. It is unclear if he's aware of what is going on. As I start to turn away, there's a subtle flicker of his eyes directed solely for my attention. It is only there for a nanosecond, but it speaks volumes. I'm sure no one else saw it but I did. It was simple and eloquent. It says, I don't know your flesh but that man means to kill you. Stick close to your new chum.

He then quite deliberately spills a trickle of beer on to the wooden boards on the floor.

Norm seems to sense something. He shifts on his bar stool and levers himself upright.

"Gotta syphon me python," he announces and lurches towards the rear.

I follow, and again I catch a flicker from the eye of the Aboriginal guy. It seems to say, she'll be right mate.

It is fiercely hot outside, and the odour in the dunny is ripening nicely. I stand next to Norm; we both unbutton our flies and let rip. There is a sound like Niagara Falls and an enormous sense of relief. When I finish Norm is still going strong, giving a passable imitation of a fire hose trying to put out a bush fire.

When we finish, we wander back indoors.

"I bet that's a weight off your mind," this from Brenda who has now finished her racing selection and is sparking up another cigarette. As I look at her, I see that she has been applying some lipstick, quite inexpertly as it happens. Indeed, it looks as though she has gone a few rounds with Johnny Famechon, the Frankston Fury who had, until relatively recently, been Aussie's own world light heavyweight boxing champion. "Jack," she drawls giving me what I thought might be her version of a come hither look, "I've got a lovely bunch of snags."

I have no idea what she is talking about, but before I can stop myself, I reply, "I'm sure you have."

Norm chokes and sprays beer all over the counter.

Brenda gives him a filthy look, and then reaches into a very large handbag and pulls out a string of rather tired pork sausages.

She whispers in a very loud voice, "Come back to ours mate and have some tea. You can watch the footy with Norm and..." there was a pause, "we'll introduce you to Gerda."

Then, in a clearly audible aside, "We are only inviting you, Jack, not that miserable mongrel," and points her cigarette towards Scarabelli.

We have time for just two more beers before staggering out into the sun.

In the car park, the tarmac is already soft. A hot breeze is picking up and, from a distance, I become aware of an intermittent crackling noise, rather like fireworks.

"The boys at the rifle club letting off steam," Brenda explains.

At the car, Norm is in a bit of trouble. He is leaning at an odd angle and has somehow managed to get his right hand stuck in his left hand trouser pocket. His flies are still undone.

His face is a picture of concentration. His tongue pokes the corner of his mouth and he is muttering almost unintelligibly, however, at one point I hear him say, "Come here," and then, "got you, you little bastard," before his hand emerges flourishing the car key.

He then proceeds to try and unlock the door. By this stage he is giving a passable impersonation of a circus contortionist. He is bent double, one hand on the car roof to steady himself, his eye to the lock while with his other hand he is painfully trying to insert the key.

After three attempts, Brenda gives up on him. She walks around the car and delivers an uppercut the Frankston Fury would have been proud of, unlocks the door and drags Norm round to the passenger seat.

I am just getting into the rear when two things happen. First, Norm re-emerges from the car holding a rifle and, clearly feeling that he is missing out on the action taking place at the rifle club, starts blazing away at the insulators on a nearby telegraph pole. Unfortunately, Norm is putting us all in danger and, when he nearly shoots his own toe off, I feel rather alarmed.

But what I see next worries me even more, Scarabelli emerging from the pub struggling with the Aboriginal guy.

Brenda doesn't see this, but she notices the worried look on my face.

Without a word she launches a sweeping haymaker which catches Norm just under the ear. He falls back, firing a final bullet as he does so. I feel it whistle past my cheek before I dive into the back seat.

As we drive away, I wonder just how long it will be before Scarabelli is back on my trail. Truth be told though, he wasn't going to be going anywhere any time soon. He lay, cold as a stoat, killed; shot right between the eyes, as the police said later, by a professional hitman.

Chapter 20:
Meanwhile, back in Rainbow

Ross woke early. The house was surprisingly quiet. He figured out that, for once, I hadn't fallen over anything when I came in the previous night, and given the silence from my bedroom, he assumed that I was still fast asleep. He helped himself to breakfast and set off early for work. He had a pile of marking to do before the school day began and, as he was leaving, he called out to my empty room, "See you later mate."

At break time Toby O'Brien came into the staff room.

"What's up with Tommo then?"

Ross shot him a puzzled look.

Toby went on, "He didn't come in this morning."

Ross thought quickly and decided to cover for me.

"He must have had a few too many yabbies last night. I reckon he's crook and decided to take a sicky."

When Ross returned home late in the afternoon, he could see immediately that I hadn't been home all day. My bedroom door was still closed so he knocked and then stepped gingerly inside and was greeted, as he said later, by an appalling sight. He later told the police that the room looked as though the bomb had hit it. I have to admit that I thought this was a bit of an exaggeration because, looking at the images that were shown in the press, it was pretty much how I'd left it the previous evening.

Ross began wondering where I could be, and the cogs in his brain began to engage and power forward. He thought it odd that my car was missing but, then again, that didn't necessarily mean much. At first, he figured that I had probably nipped off to Melbourne for a couple of days without telling anyone, but when he found my passport on my bedside table he was puzzled. He only became alarmed, however, when he found the bloodstained T-shirt on my bedroom floor. He was now beginning to get a bad feeling but, telling himself not to panic, he went into town to look for me. He did the rounds of my usual haunts but to no avail. On the way back he bumped into the school secretary.

"G'day, I'm looking for Tommo. Have you seen him around?"

She thought for a moment. "Yeah, yesterday arvo. I gave him a note from some Italian bloke staying at the Golden Nugget."

His mind went into overdrive. He began to put things together. Each piece of the jigsaw was beginning to create a terrible whole. The visit of a mysterious stranger, my recent behaviour in the chemistry lab, my disappearance and the bloodstained T-shirt all seemed to add up to something that might be very unpleasant, if not downright sinister. To calm himself he did the obvious thing, calling in at the Eureka Hotel and downing a couple of cold ones. Eventually, at around 9pm, he gave in to his concerns, ordered another beer, sculled it in one go, walked to the payphone and put in a missing person call in to the Commonwealth Police. Within an hour an officer was on the scene, and by midnight he had factored into my disappearance some additional information including my recent visit to Victoria Market and the discovery that Mr. Scarabelli, late of the Golden Nugget, had a colourful criminal record punctuated by acts of extreme violence.

Someone, I'm not sure who, must have tipped off the news desk at the Jeparit Bugle, because the next day's edition carried the first published account of my disappearance.

Teacher disappears
Signs of a violent struggle

Concerns were first raised about 4pm yesterday after school teacher Tommo Wilson failed to report for work.

His housemate and a fellow teacher Ross Tyler said, 'It's unlike Tommo, he's Mister Reliable. His car's gone but his passport and most of his clothes are still here. I'm really worried.'

Mr. Wilson, who is said to be from England, arrived in Rainbow only a few weeks ago. Stan Kemp, who runs the general store, told the Bugle that Mr. Wilson was already well known in town as an amateur horse racing tipster and keen follower of Aussie rules football. 'I can only imagine that he must have had some gambling problems or something. He kept it quiet, but I could tell immediately that he was a keen punter, in fact I'd go so far as to say that I reckon that he might have been addicted to the ponies.'

A police spokesman said 'We have serious concerns for Mr. Wilson's safety. We have reason to believe that he was involved in a violent struggle at his home and there is evidence of that struggle continuing outside the building. Anyone who saw Mr. Wilson or who has any information regarding his whereabouts should contact the police immediately. At this moment in time, we have no further information to share with the public.'

An unconfirmed source said that bloodstained clothing belonging to Mr. Wilson had been found at the house he was sharing with Mr. Tyler. A wider search of the area revealed a trail of blood leading to the grain silos on the outskirts of the town. It is understood that another item belonging to Mr. Wilson, possibly a house key, was found at that location.

Local Head Teacher, Toby O'Brien, said, 'We are all in a state of shock. I know that Tommo was training hard for this weekend's footy game and has talked of little else for the past couple of weeks. He's a keen member of the team and I don't think he'd miss it for quids. I'm really quite concerned.'

Locals, who did not wish to be named, have linked Mr. Wilson's disappearance to the arrival in town of businessmen from both Melbourne and Adelaide.

In a possibly related development, local greengrocer Mario Lucarelli has been admitted to Jeparit bush hospital suffering from multiple injuries. He is said to be in a serious but stable condition.

Police stress that, despite rumours to the contrary, they have no reason to believe that either Mr. Wilson or Mr. Lucarelli are connected in any way to underworld figures who are said to have visited Rainbow recently.

Later that day a TV crew checked in to the Golden Nugget, and news of the disappearance soon began popping up on national bulletins.

Chapter 21:
Once in a lifetime

Greg Pritchard was having a hell of a day. As editor, reporter and owner of the Jeparit Bugle, things had never been so exciting. For once, folks were actually reading the stuff he wrote.

Greg knew this was his big opportunity to make his mark as a hot shot reporter. What he now needed was to market the story, to give it a brand. He needed to give it a headline that would grab everyone's attention. This was the moment he'd been waiting for, a chance to get a return on his investment in that creative writing course he'd done all those years ago at Horsham Tech College.

He padded round the office and then decided to do what he always did when stuck for a bit of copy. He rolled a spliff, slid his favourite compilation tape into the cassette deck, heard the satisfying clunk as it engaged and then he hit the play button. Greg sat back, inhaled deeply, and waited for the muse to visit.

'Once in a Lifetime' poured from the speakers. Greg smiled. He loved this track. Especially the lines:

And you may find yourself in another part of the world
And you may find yourself behind the wheel of a large automobile
And you may ask yourself, "Well, how did I get here?"

Greg dreamed of being that man in the large automobile, living in another part of the world, Geelong perhaps or Ballarat, as a reporter on a much bigger newspaper than the Bugle. Perhaps this breaking story was his big chance, his once in a lifetime opportunity.

He inhaled deeply and waited.

It was 'Psycho Killer' that did the trick. Greg at first thought the words were 'Silo Killer' and the more he listened and the more he smoked, the better it sounded.

He pulled a big fat marker pen from a drawer and in big black letters wrote a headline on a large piece of butcher paper.

SILO KILLER

He liked that. He also liked the next line. So, he wrote that down as well,

Qu'est ce que c'est?

Greg looked at his creation and smiled.

SILO KILLER. Qu'est ce que c'est?

It was a work of genius. There was just one problem. The cockies would have no idea what the hell 'Qu'est ce que c'est?' meant.

He screwed up the paper and threw it in the bin.

He scrawled another headline, simpler this time,

SILO KILLER?

Yeah, that was better. Simpler, more to the point. But, on reflection, a bit weak, a bit tentative,

He needed something more direct, more emphatic, more dramatic. Perhaps a little more prosaic. And then he had it,

RAINBOW KILLER?

Greg felt pleased and then began polishing his work of art. It still wasn't quite right. Greg deleted the question mark. It became **RAINBOW KILLER** and then **THE RAINBOW KILLER**. Greg liked the word '**THE**'. It seemed to add weight. Then with a final flourish he added the coup de grace because, after all, there could be more than one killer.

THE RAINBOW KILLERS

Greg felt pleased, so pleased that he rolled another spliff. As he inhaled, he began dreaming. He was in Melbourne, floating down Lygon Street where the upwardly mobile literati were sipping their expensive Italian coffees. As his reverie deepened, he began to revisit the headline. Somehow, it wasn't sophisticated enough. He needed something that might attract a wider audience. He went back to the waste bin and retrieved the piece of paper he had thrown away earlier. He smoothed it out on his desk and looked at it with pleasure.

"Bollocks to the cockies," he said to the empty office. "They can take it or leave it."

So, that is how the following day's issue of the Bugle carried the headline which would put Rainbow on the map, kick off Greg Pritchard's career and spawn a dozen books and a couple of TV specials:

SILO KILLER Qu'est ce que c'est?

Chapter 22:
A bloody mess

The scene at the Wellshot Hotel was, as Inspector Kettle said, a bloody mess. The shooting had happened in plain sight and on his patch and yet no one had seen a thing. In fact, no one was quite sure of the exact timing of the death of the stranger.

The only clues were the cars. A yellow Holden and a wrecked Valiant, the latter found a couple of miles down the road. Both had out of state plates. Clearly the killer was related to one of the cars and the murderer to the other.

A few quick calls identified that the Valiant was registered to a missing person from somewhere called Rainbow and the Holden belonged to an Italian family in Melbourne.

The Valiant, however, contained a clue. A caravan site sticker on the wrecked windshield had a very recent date and suggested that the driver had stopped for a night in Rockhampton. Inspector Kettle felt instinctively that the identity of that driver was the key to this puzzle. The pieces were falling neatly into place and, with just a few more phone calls, Inspector Kettle was sure he would soon have the answer. Time was of the essence. It always was in murder cases. He had to work fast.

Chapter 23:
Gerda, Brutus and the mummy

I'm having a nightmare. In it I see someone encased from head to foot in plaster and, as he sees me, there's a moment of recognition before he screams in terror.

I jolt awake. I'm hot and very sticky. Next to me is a crushed can of beer and a bowl half full of what looks like Heinz Cream of Vegetable soup. I'm confused and take a sniff, and that's all I need to begin retching once more.

In the kitchen, Norm is padding about wearing a pair of small, tight fitting stubbies and smoking a roll up. For someone in my delicate condition this is not a pleasant sight.

The TV is roaring full blast. It's an ad for Mellox Worming tablets. Then there's a plug for something called Ringer's Shag. When the programme resumes, it's a helicopter image of a small collection of buildings and a car park. In the shot there's a small group of people and a couple of police cars.

"Jeez we missed all the fun last night," Norm drawls, "There was a shooting at the pub."

I instinctively reach out for the TV and up the volume. Partly masked by the whirring of helicopter blades and the sound of Norm gargling and spitting into the sink I make out the words 'Scarabelli…. Melbourne Mafia'. And then a local reporter called Greg Pritchard talking about someone he calls 'The Silo Killer'. There's an aerial shot of Rainbow accompanied by a voice-over, 'Police are convinced this was a professional hit. Underworld sources suggest the killer is Jack Nicholson, also wanted…'

The flyscreen door bursts open and in struts a muscular woman with matted blonde hair. She too is wearing tight stubbies, but fortunately also sports a T-shirt. It was probably once white but it is now grey in colour, decorated with spots of dried blood, with a yellow trim under the armpits. She immediately reminds me of someone I've seen hurling a discus on that TV programme, *A Question of Sport*. I figure that she's the farm hand Norm and Brenda mentioned on the way back last night.

"You're up then," she says and flashes an unforgettable smile, reminiscent of those images you see of Berlin after the war, all lopsided buildings and collapsed masonry. I immediately see a possible reason for this dental chaos as she seems to be sucking on a gobstopper, all the while chasing a sliver of drool which is threatening to escape down her chin. She proffers a rough and bloody hand "G'day, I'm Gerda. You'll be Jack. Heard all about you. Just been out castrating the lambs." She smiles, reaches into her pocket and pulls out a spherical red object. "Wanna try sucking on this?"

It wasn't the last time she'd offer me a gobstopper.

As I step out onto the front porch I'm confronted by a cyclone of snarling teeth, dog phlegm and fur. I've inadvertently woken Brutus, a beast almost the size of a Shetland pony who looks like a cross between a Dobermann Pinscher and the Hound of the Baskervilles. Fortunately, he is tethered by a very large gauge steel chain, having just wolfed a large zinc bucketful of sheep's testicles.

"Settle down Brutus. He's beaut ain't he?" - this from Brenda who has just been out to "throttle a couple of chooks for tucker tonight."

"We got him cheap. Thirty bucks, not bad for a thoroughbred. They said he had a bad temper, but as long as you don't upset him, he's normally as nice as pie. Mind you, if he saw anyone attacking me, Norm or Gerda he'd kill 'em."

I don't doubt it for a moment. Brenda clocks my expression, smiles approvingly and continues, "By the way, I wouldn't stand like that if I were you."

"Like what?" I ask.

"You know, with your..." Brenda was searching for the right word. I think she was trying to be delicate. "With your, er, your er knackers facing him. He'll take it as a threat and, like as not, try to rip 'em off."

That afternoon I went out on a quad bike. Gerda had offered to show me the sights. She shifted forward onto the driver's seat and said in an ambiguous tone, "Climb on board and grab hold of anything you fancy." I took this as a joke but, looking back, perhaps I should have given the invitation more consideration. Quite what I was expecting I'm not sure, but after driving across an almost barren landscape for about ten minutes, we pulled up by a solitary tree. "Get down!" Gerda barked. I think this was supposed to be an invitation, but it seemed more like an order. She disappeared behind the trunk and emerged seconds later naked apart from her heavy duty work boots. "Fancy doin' a bit of sunbaking?" she asked. Before I could answer, she pushed me to the floor and sat astride my chest. I heard her whisper "Jack, you're so forward." My brain was trying to process this but was having difficulty as I felt as though I was being crushed to death and was about to black out when her tongue forced its way into my mouth, followed immediately by a saliva covered, half eaten, gobstopper. As I struggled, literally fighting for my life, Gerda seemed to take it as a sign of enthusiasm. I heard her say, "Stop it Jack," and then her mouth was on my neck and I felt a really painful series of bites and was sure my carotid artery was about to be punctured. My struggling only seemed to encourage Gerda. She swivelled surprisingly deftly and began yanking off my trousers. At this point I really must have lost consciousness because the next thing I remember is a hot wet mouth moving its way up my thigh. That mouth, however, didn't belong to Gerda because, when I came to, she was running towards me from the quad bike armed with a cattle prod. The mouth belonged to Brutus.

I'm recovering in the kitchen, still shaking. On my left buttock is a burn mark where Gerda accidentally electrocuted me. Brutus, meanwhile, is literally and physically in the doghouse, chained up in the machine shed. Apparently, to get him off me Gerda had to give him four or five jolts from the prod, and it has made him really unhappy. As a result, Norm has taken what I think is a wise decision, to lace his food with horse tranquiliser until he 'settles down'.

Not content with murdering the chooks once, Brenda has proceeded to cook them in a unique way. She calls it 'good old outback tucker', I call it burnt on the outside and raw in the middle. I try to eat as I don't want to offend the chef, but I'm finding it difficult.

Fortunately, everyone is distracted by the theme tune of the early evening news blaring out from the TV. The lead story is again the hunt for the hitman who iced Maurizio Scarabelli. The police are no further forward in pursuing their enquiries, and the mysterious Mr. Nicholson has apparently disappeared without a trace. I think even Norm might have started to add things up had it not been for the fact that Scarabelli had been alive when we left the pub, but I can tell something is troubling him.

The next item is from interstate. It's about the victim of a gangland beating. Brenda reaches over to change channels. "We saw this last night, dontcha remember? I wanna watch the trots on the other side." I didn't remember seeing anything last night. All I could recall was that after we got back to Norm's place, we opened up a quart bottle of Bundaberg and heroically demolished it.

Norm grabs Brenda's hand, "Hold yer flaming horses for a minute. I wanna see the footy scores."

We carry on watching the news. The footage seems vaguely familiar. Maybe we had seen it last night. I stare. A man encased almost totally in plaster and lying immobile is being interviewed. The story begins, 'Rainbow greengrocer Mario Lucarelli is believed to have been the victim of a mob related punishment beating. Meanwhile the search goes on for local school teacher, Tommo Wilson. Police would not confirm rumours that Wilson was involved in the Melbourne drug trade.'

A rather portly police officer then appears on screen. 'We are still treating this as a missing persons case, but the fact that Mr. Wilson left without telling anyone where he was going makes us fear for his safety.'

Norm belches and opens another flagon of Mudgee Mud. "He's gorn. I reckon he's dogmeat by now."

At around ten o'clock the phone rings. The evening trots have finished and Brenda seems pleased. Two winners and a place. It's been a long day and no one is keen to answer. I'm about to turn in so, on my way, I pick it up.

"How ya doin' yer old bastard?" I recognise the voice. Its Lance, the barman at the Wellshot Hotel. And he needs a word with 'Norm or his Missus'.

I pass the phone to Norm. There then follows a long conversation.

Norm seems concerned and finishes the call saying, "Don't worry mate, thanks for the heads up, Brutus will take care of us if there's any trouble."

When he sits down, we all look at him.

Gerda asks, "is there a problem?"

"Not sure. There's some bloke been asking for you Jack, says his name is Lenny Landolpho, that ring any bells?"

Yeah it did, alarm bells. The name sounded too Italian to be a coincidence, and I couldn't help but think he was connected to Mr. Scarabelli's business interests.

I needed to make a move, and quick.

Chapter 24:
Brutus' story

I have to say it's been a bit of a day, and I must admit I've seen better ones.

Waking up with a head full of horse tranquiliser and an arse scorched by several jolts from the cattle prod was bad enough, but finding that Norm had chained me up was the icing on a very unpleasant piece of cake.

Now, we all know that humans are dim, right? I mean they have to be. I've managed to con them for years into feeding me and providing a roof over my head, and all I have to do is threaten to savage anyone who comes within fifty yards of the place. Meanwhile they chase around doing something they call work. They spend a lot of time talking about work and mainly the chat is about how much they hate it.

Work, in fact, seems, in fact to dominate their lives. All dogs know this. I mean we aren't stupid. We've figured out that us just jumping up and trying to sniff their groins seems to make humans happy, and usually takes their minds off work. I say usually, because sometimes you have to do a bit more – like pissing on the curtains for example or, if work seems to be going really badly, taking a dump in the kitchen while they are preparing food. Don't get me wrong, I've never actually done any of these things myself but it's what my old mucker, a street fighter called Mingus, told me once when I was bailed up in the Footscray dog pound. Come to think of it, maybe that's why Mingus was out on the streets in the first place.

Anyway, let's get back to what happened today. At about midday Gerda came to feed me. Yeuch, testicles again. I don't know how many times I've told them that they're not good for me. And, unless they are even dumber than I give them credit for, they should know it too, because they watched the same *Horizon* documentary on the effects of excess testosterone as I did. Admittedly, Gerda fell asleep part way through and Norm drank about half a bottle of rum during the proceedings, and Brenda was perhaps a little side tracked by her knitting, but even so, the bottom line was crystal clear: too much testosterone makes you, shall we say, a little edgy? Oh, and if that's not bad enough, what about the horse tranquiliser? You'd think they would all know better because we all sat and watched that clip on the news. You know the one, the one about grizzly bears in Yellowstone National Park who were rounded up, pumped full of drugs and dropped by helicopter miles from anywhere, only to go and eat a few humans when they woke up. You only have to be able to add two and two to figure out that this stuff doesn't actually tranquilise anything. What is does is paralyse you and, when you wake up, as like as not it sends you into a paranoid rage and makes you want to eat people. I can't read very well, but I'm pretty certain it says that on the label. If it doesn't it should. I'm just telling you that by way of an aside, so you don't really blame me for what went on this afternoon.

Now, when Gerda set me free, I was feeling sore at both ends. The burns on my rear were playing up and the horse tranquiliser was doing strange things to my head. To make matters worse I was as hot as hell and had a strange craving for raw flesh, human if possible. I thought for a moment that I might try sneaking a chunk out of that Pommy bloke, Jack, but given what happened yesterday, I thought better of it. I decided instead to prowl the boundary fence alongside the road into town and lie in wait for a kangaroo. That would have to do.

On my way I stopped by a sheep trough and stuck my head in,

way underwater. It was cool and refreshing there, and kind of weird in a pleasant sort of way. I gazed at the sunbeams filtering through the water and drifted into a beautiful dream. I was a puppy again, well bred, good tempered and loved by my owners. I'd forgotten, but now I recalled that in those days my name was different. I was, wait for it…Derek. Derek! — what sort of a name is that? I wondered — but this thought was instantly overlaid by the warm memory of my mother calling to me in dog language, "Derek, it's time to eat". I don't know whether it was the drugs but I was in dog heaven, a feeling which persisted until I passed out through lack of oxygen and was only saved by the fact that, as I keeled over, I tipped the trough upside down.

I must have lain in the dust for quite a while before I recovered consciousness. Indeed, for a few minutes afterwards I was convinced that I was dead, only to realise, when an ugly bot fly bit me on the rear, that I was still alive.

I was still feeling peculiar when I got to the fence and was glad to find some long grass to lie down in. In a few minutes I was asleep again, I think that the drugs were still careering round my system. This time the dreams were not at all pleasant. It was all of a jumble, and painful to relate. Over and over again my mind replayed the moment I was separated from my mother. I didn't even have time to say goodbye before a lead was put around my neck and I was driven off towards the big city. Within two days I had escaped, which in retrospect was not a smart move because that led me to become a street dog, a fighting dog, and ultimately to the dog pound. How I got out of there is a whole other story, but let's just say it involved a gang of crazed loons led by someone the dogs in the pound called Mystic Trev. About every full moon, Mystic Trev and his mates would break in at dead of night and unloose dog hell. Usually about thirty or forty dogs would be liberated before the so called security guards managed to restore some sort of order. Mystic Trev was a legend and I owe him, because one glorious night Mingus and I were woken from our dreams and led to freedom through a freshly made hole in the chain link fence and, since tasting the fresh air of freedom, I've been determined that I will never, ever return to that hell hole again. My escape was tinged with sadness. I never saw Mingus again. The dogs on the street say he left with Mystic Trev, others say he was totalled by a truck somewhere near Ballarat. I guess we'll probably never know the truth.

Now don't get me wrong, living with Norm and Brenda is a breeze compared to some of the places I've been. After all, they treat me well, but, and I have difficulty saying this, our intellectual interests are not quite the same. You see I really like historical dramas and science programmes but, unless everyone is asleep or drunk, most of what we get is footy or the trots. Sometimes I feel that life is passing me by out here.

Anyway, it was while I was dozing in the grass reflecting on all this that the tranquiliser terrors began to creep up on me. You know what I mean; it always hits sooner or later once you've had a dose of the old donkey dropper. Somewhere in your subconscious the feeling of unease builds until you know with absolute certainty that something awful is going to happen. The only problem is, even when you wake up you can't move, the drugs have got you paralysed again, and you just have to lie still hoping for things to blow over. I guess, and it's only just come to me, that's what people mean when they talk about lying doggo.

This is probably the most dangerous time to encounter anyone, or anything, who has had a massive dose of horse tranquiliser. They are frightened and, quite naturally, can become aggressive. It was, therefore, quite unlucky timing for the stranger in the black sedan who had parked up by the fence. He was looking at the house through a pair of field glasses. In my paranoid state of mind I was sure he was looking for me, so I decided to keep quiet and watch what he was up to.

My vigil was disturbed by the sound of the screen door opening and then slamming. Back at the house, I noticed Jack limping gingerly out towards the dunny. The stranger went back to the car and pulled something out of the boot. I know now what it was he had in his hand, but in my fevered state I was sure it was a cattle prod. I felt the fur on my neck bristle with fear, and then the man did something most unexpected. He rested the prod against the fence, unzipped his fly and started marking MY territory. All of a sudden I was consumed by fear, anger and an undeniable craving for human flesh.

Apart from the eating, it was all over in a matter of seconds. It was Norm who discovered the crime. Strangely, he didn't use the cattle prod on me. He just vomited and then started swearing. He gave me a few strange looks and used the F word quite a lot and then he picked up the stick the man had been carrying. My mind must have been clearing because I saw for the first time it was a gun, not your ordinary sort of gun, but one like the one we saw last week in that film about the bloke who was supposed to have shot that politician in the US. It was sleek, and topped off with what Norm described later to Jack as a telescopic sight.

I was expecting trouble, but Norm patted me on the head, fastened the heavy chain round my collar and led me back to the machine shed. He didn't say a word.

I slept most of the rest of the day, lulled to sleep by the whirring of the mincing machine next door. That night I ate in the shed alone.

Somehow, I could tell that Norm and Brenda had something on their minds and that something had to do with Jack 'taking care' of me and someone called Lenny Landolpho. I knew from the TV that to take care of someone could mean different things to different people, and I wondered for a while if they were going to pull that 'happy farm' stunt on me. You know the one, the one parents always tell the kids when the dog has just torn up the new carpet. "We've decided to take Brutus to live on a farm where they will take care of him. He will be happy there, there are lots of rabbits for him to chase and he will love it." What a crock. But what they really mean is, Brutus is a pain in the butt and is going to be given a lethal injection at Crippen's veterinary practice down the road.

So, when dinner arrived I was more than a tad nervous when I realised it wasn't testicles. It smelt and tasted familiar, rather like something I had eaten before, not so long ago. Nevertheless, I wolfed it down. What the hell, I thought, if I'm in for that big doggy walk in the sky it's no use fretting. After all what was it that Italian bloke on the TV sang, *Que sera sera?* Something about that singer chimed not only with my sense of destiny, but also with my taste buds. Surely my last meal on earth wasn't an Italian, was it?

Chapter 25:
Kangaroo Pete

It was Gerda who got to the point first, "We've got to get rid of the evidence."

By evidence, she didn't mean the body. Brutus was already taking care of that. What she meant was the black limousine, the rifle and whatever else Lenny Landolpho had been carrying with him.

Although it was only about eight o'clock in the morning, Norm's singlet was already drenched in sweat as he opened the fridge, ripped open a can and took a long pull of Castlemaine XXXX.

"We've got to get it to the crusher and bloody quick before the rest of the Italian cavalry arrives."

Brenda looked up. "Crusher, my arse. That car's worth a few bob. I reckon we could drop it off at Kangaroo Pete's and no one will be any the wiser."

Although I had no idea who Kangaroo Pete was, Brenda was clearly on the ball and had been thinking ahead. "Jack, you need to go out of here and quick, so why not kill two birds with one stone; take the car, steal a march on whoever is after you, and leave us in the clear?" She took a long pull on her cigarette, "Oh, and another thing. While you're about it, it might be a good idea if you took care of Brutus as well." I could tell by the expression on her face that the sort of care she wanted me to administer to Brutus was not a short term fix, but of a permanent variety, if you get my drift.

We were mulling things over when the phone rang. We looked at each other, fearing the worst. Surely it couldn't be the Italians again could it?

Gerda picked up the receiver and listened intently. The voice on the other end spoke for a couple of minutes. I strained to try and pick up what was being said, but just caught the odd snatch including, the words 'horseflesh' and 'deadweight' and then almost at the end 'he pulled his head off and got slaughtered'.

"Struth," Brenda looked distinctly upset. There was silence for a few moments and I felt an urgent need to visit the dunny.

Norm was the first to speak, "What's the damage?"

Brenda looked up, took another drag and replied, "Seventy-five bucks down the shitter. The bloody jockey didn't know the horse's arse from its apex."

I breathed a sigh of relief. The call had been from the local bookmakers informing Brenda of the performance of her latest investment in the sport of kings. The incident had, however, focused our minds. The next call might not be from a friendly local bookie, it might be from friends of the late Mr. Landolpho, so we clearly did not have time to lose.

It took about ten minutes to empty the car and load my gear. Everyone seemed to have been energised by the phone call, and I'm sure that I was not the only one who was constantly scanning the horizon for unwanted visitors.

As I climbed aboard, Gerda gave me a smile and a gobstopper. "This car stands out like a dingo's donger. Just drive and don't stop for anything, and be careful."

I thought I was going to get clean away, but Brenda saw what I was up to and dragged Brutus up to the car and dumped him in the front seat.

Norm handed something to me, a paint tin filled with ground meat. "When you stop just give him this". I knew from Norm's expression that there was a secret ingredient, and that this was

Brutus's last meal. "Bye, you old bastard," with a tear in his eye, he gave the dog a hug.

I climbed aboard, gunned the engine and headed northwest into the great beyond.

Gerda was right about the car. It was impressive, a Ford Falcon muscle car, jet black with smoked windows and an engine noise that resembled a wild beast with a hangover. The car rolled along the blacktop eating the miles while all the time I kept a weather eye out for vehicles in my rear view mirror.

A couple of hours beyond Longreach, I decided it was time to say a last farewell to Brutus. He'd been quiet for the whole journey, so I guess he pretty much knew what was coming. I was looking for a place to do it, and found the right spot a few miles shy of Winton in the shade of a large billboard which said *Welcome to the Diamantina*, and underneath in smaller letters, *Get your Diamantina Cocktail at the Winton Hotel - 10 miles*.

I suppose I'm telling all this because I want to distract you from what happened next. So, if you'll excuse me, I'll gloss over the details. Just take it from me that I was as gentle as I could be, and that as I got back into the car I had, for some unknown reason, a lump in my throat.

Almost as soon as I pulled back onto the highway I noticed, in the rear view mirror, the glint of sun on glass as a bright yellow car moved into sight. Even though I didn't really think that anyone would be on my trail I stepped on to the gas and, as the speedo climbed towards the hundred mark, I began to leave the other vehicle behind.

The town of Winton looked something like a scene from a Russell Drysdale painting: wide open spaces, burning streets and muted colours bleached by the sun, accompanied by an overwhelming sense of distance and loneliness.

Kangaroo Pete's place was just off the quiet main street in a large block surrounded by corrugated iron fencing and topped with barbed wire. I got the impression that it didn't see much business. A local artist had painted a hoarding displaying an image of a boxing kangaroo with the legends *Kangaroo Pete won't be beat*, and *Cheap spares. Best prices paid for scrap metal.*

I drove in and parked up by a mountain of flattened vehicles, most of which looked as if they had been there for decades. I switched the engine off and got out.

I don't know whether you've ever tried looking for a needle in a haystack, but I reckon you'd have more luck finding one than you would of ever finding a replacement gearbox or head gasket in Pete's scrap yard. If you've seen those Don McCullin photographs of the citadel of Hue after the Tet offensive you'll have an idea of the layout: twisted steel, rubble and chaos everywhere, all gently turning to dust in the outback heat.

I made my way between overhanging piles of metal, following handwritten signs to the office, a wooden shack decorated with faded images from girlie magazines. On the table was a telephone that had once been cream in colour but now was covered in black greasy fingerprints. Sitting behind a table in an armchair that looked as though it had been savaged by the Hound of the Baskervilles was Kangaroo Pete. I recognised him at once, not because I had ever seen him before, but because of the large kangaroo shaped strawberry birthmark on his cheek. He was wearing black footy shorts and a torn singlet, and looked like a professional mud wrestler. Curiously, he was deep in concentration, reading a book by some Russian bloke. It was aptly entitled *Crime and Punishment*.

He smiled and, in doing so, exposed his teeth which reminded me, in an odd way, of that horror movie, *Nightmare on Elm Street*.

Pete shot me a knowing look. "G'day, I've been expecting you. Norm's been on the blower, reckons we need to be quick, 'cos he's had company. Said you'd know what he meant."

I handed him the keys to the Falcon.

"Better have a quick look at her."

We walked to the car and Pete gave it a cursory inspection. He turned the ignition, listened to the engine and, seeming satisfied, rolled it into a workshop where he covered it with a heavy tarp.

We walked back to the office. I don't know whether he was talking to me or to himself, but he was mumbling something about a spray job, new plates and 'fixing the rego papers'. He then picked up the phone and dialled a number. A few seconds later I heard Norm pick it up at the other end and then hand the phone to Brenda. I wasn't really listening but gathered that Pete was going to pay a couple of thousand bucks for the car and get rid of any evidence linking it to its previous owner. It seemed like a good deal all round, especially when Pete told me that, as part of the deal, he would also sort me out with some wheels and cash to help me make good my escape.

He was about to hang up when Brenda said something. Pete frowned and handed the phone to me.

Brenda sounded agitated and a little scared. "They've been here, looking for you Jack. We told them that you'd shot through. They are also looking for, er, Landolpho." She said the last word in a low voice. "I reckon you need to move, and fast, the further the better. Darwin's nice I reckon."

DARWIN? Jesus H Christ. NICE? It must be hotter than hell at this time of year. Probably pissing with rain as well. But, thinking about it, there didn't seem much choice. Either I ploughed on and tried to outrun the mob, or I retraced my steps.

I was just weighing things up when a yellow car rolled into the yard.

Pete reached into a desk drawer and pulled out a dull metal object which he placed on the desk - a sawn-off shotgun. The sun hammered down and we waited in the shadows for our visitor to announce himself.

The driver got out, stretched his legs, and sparked up a cigarette. He looked as though he meant business.

Chapter 26:
The stranger

The stranger wandered around the yard and then sauntered into the office.

"G'day," he said, "I'm looking for a bloke driving a black Falcon. Folks down the street said he might've come in here."

Kangaroo Pete was playing it cool.

"We get heaps of folks in here."

I thought this might be stretching things a bit, but Pete went on,

"I reckon we had a black Falcon last week, didn't we?"

Kangaroo Pete gestured to me and I nodded.

"Nah, I'm talking about today. Are you sure you haven't seen him?"

I shook my head and Pete replied for us both,

"Look, it's a small town, if this bloke is around here, he shouldn't be hard to spot. We can pass on a message for you." It was at this moment that the stranger clocked the gun on Pete's desk.

His body language changed immediately, and he began slowly edging out of the door.

Pete raised himself from the chair.

"Hold your flamin horses. Before you go, I want to know why you are looking for this bloke."

The stranger started to shake.

I was all ears.

"I don't want any trouble, it's just that I've got something of his. I just wanted to do the right thing. A couple of miles back I saw him pull out of a parking place and then I saw this dog chasing the car down the road. I figured that the driver had forgotten him and I just wanted to …. bring him back."

Pete shot me a look and could tell from my reaction that there was some mileage in the story.

The stranger moved backwards, carefully into the sun towards his car. He opened the rear door and stepped aside. Pete followed his every movement, gun in hand, not taking any chances.

I stared into the back and there, lying spark out, was Brutus who, not much more than an hour ago, I had simply abandoned to fend for himself.

As I moved to lift him Brutus woke and leaped at me, smothering my face with slobber. He seemed genuinely pleased to see me and, in an odd way, I was kind of glad that we had been reunited. The stranger seemed pleased as well but, for some reason, was in an indecent hurry to get away.

By the time Kangaroo Pete had fixed me up with the replacement car he had promised, the day was drawing to a close. Not only did he give me the keys to an old Datsun, but he handed me an envelope containing about a hundred dollars. Enough to get me as far as Darwin, about thirteen hundred miles away, if I was careful with the cash.

I lay that night in my swag under the stars some way down the road out towards Mount Isa. Knowing that people were still chasing me meant I was still running scared. After Darwin I had no plan. It was enough for the moment just to get there and get away from here. It seemed to be the story of my life. The fact that Brutus lay sleeping silently beside me gave me some comfort, and, as I was drifting off into a fitful sleep I recall thinking that he seemed to have undergone some sort of character change since joining me on my flight to freedom, and I had an odd thought that perhaps Brutus realised that, in a way, he was also running away from something. I also began to wonder when, if ever, we'd both be running towards something.

As you may have deduced, I never did get my Diamantina cocktail and, perhaps it's just as well, seeing as how I later discovered that it is an ungodly mixture of Bundaberg Rum and condensed milk, topped off with an emu's egg.

Chapter 27:
Fatal attraction

The stench of death and decay was so strong that for a while afterwards, I felt that it was actually stuck to my skin. At first, I thought that it might have been something that Brutus's alimentary tract had been processing but, in reality, it was far worse than that.

It took me some time to figure out that the smell was coming from road kill. As I left the dirt road and hit the tarmac the aroma was overpowering, I trundled over kangaroo after kangaroo that had been flattened into the soft bitumen. I don't know why, but this particular stretch of the highway seemed to have a fatal attraction for wildlife, although curiously I didn't see a single live animal that day.

A few miles down the road I saw a sign for the Burke and Wills memorial.

I knew the epic story well, so I pulled over.

A small obelisk, inlaid with green lumps of copper ore, was set back from the highway and bore the following inscription:

This memorial was erected by the Cloncurry Shire Council, Mt Isa Mines Ltd and Mary Kathleen Uranium Ltd to commemorate the expedition of Burke and Wills who crossed this spot on 22nd January 1861 on their journey across the Australian Continent.

I knew that in 1860–61, Robert O'Hara Burke and William Wills led an expedition across Australia. They intended to travel from Melbourne in the south to the Gulf of Carpentaria in the north, a distance of around two thousand miles. At that time most of inland Australia was completely unknown to European settlers and, as it turned out, was as dry as a cattleman's throat.

The journey was a tragedy, perhaps greater than the more famous Scott expedition to the South Pole. Burke and Wills, and companions Tom King and Charley Gray, got to within about a mile of the sea in the Gulf of Carpentaria, but were blocked by mangrove swamps. In an epic retreat they retraced their route, eating their camels as they went. Just a couple of days from what they thought was the safety of their supply depot at Cooper's Creek, Charley Gray died and they spent a day burying him. When they trooped into the depot they found that their support party had left. The three survivors must have been demoralised. Then they noticed something that could hardly have improved their spirits. The word DIG was carved into the trunk of a large gum tree and, hoping against hope, they did just that. In the tree roots they found a message in a bottle. It gave the hour and date of the support team's departure and offered a promise that they would return once they had replenished their own supplies, which had virtually run out. Burke and Wills checked the date and realised the appalling truth that they had missed their colleagues by about three hours, but even though safety was so close at hand, they were too exhausted to follow. If only they had turned up earlier they would have been safe, but now they were abandoned in one of the most inhospitable places on earth. What makes this even more tragic was the fact that, had they not stopped to bury Charley Gray, all would have ended well.

In the event, Burke and Wills died but their companion, Tom King, survived with the help of a local Aboriginal tribe until rescuers finally returned three months later. King returned to Melbourne a hero.

I was still a long way out of Mount Isa when I caught sight of its most famous landmark, the tall red and white chimney stack of the town's lead smelter, belching fumes into the otherwise clear blue sky.

I'd been told that Mount Isa had the highest levels of lead poisoning amongst children in the country and, looking at the scale of operations, that wasn't hard to believe.

In fact, I was wondering whether I'd got a case of post-traumatic stress, because stopping off to pay homage at the Burke and Wills memorial didn't seem to be too smart an idea. Every car I saw as a possible threat, and I had to force myself to get things into perspective. After all, the people who were after me didn't know what sort of car I was driving, nor did they know where I was going, so I told myself to try and loosen up. I reasoned that the more nervous I felt, the more edgy I would look and the easier I would be to spot in a crowd. I just had to try and relax.

In terms of hiding out, Mount Isa had one thing going for me. Almost everyone on the street seemed to be male and around about my age or younger.

The problem was my accent. I thought I would stand out like the proverbial spare at a wedding but, as I wandered up to 'Queen Doreen's, the Best Little Café in the West', my fears subsided. There were about twenty people eating breakfast to a conversational soundtrack that might have been recorded live at the Tower of Babel. I picked out English, German, Italian, French Egyptian and Turkish accents, all laced with an overtopping of rural Queensland. It was perfect. I tied Brutus to a lamppost and went inside.

From snatches of conversation, it seemed that almost everybody had just arrived in town, and all of them were looking for work. There was a big cardboard notice on one wall which was getting heaps of attention: *Men wanted. Skilled and unskilled positions Top wages. MIM LTD. Call Barry on 07 237533521*

I smiled. Finding me here would be like looking for a bot fly at a barbecue.

Queen Doreen, the café's owner, was a human tornado. She was a robust figure, and someone I guess you wouldn't want to mess with. She was holding the fort, yelling orders to the kitchen, taking orders, delivering food and clearing tables, all the while exchanging banter with the clientele.

"Sunny side up? I'll give you bloody sunny side up. What do you think this is, the bloody Ritz? You'll get what you're given and be glad about it."

I ordered breakfast and an extra strong cup of strong black coffee and wedged myself into a corner seat where I had a good view of the traffic, just in case. I tried telling myself that this was pointless because I had no idea what my pursuer or pursuers looked like, but some sixth sense just wouldn't let me rest.

Doreen interrupted my train of thought. "Get yer ribs round this," she ordered as she handed me my food. It was eggs and bacon, but not quite like anything I'd ever seen before. Four fried eggs, about ten rashers and a doorstop sized pile of fried bread, all topped off with tinned tomatoes. "Just yell if you need anything else," she called as she flew past, already on to the next customer.

Doreen was quite a force of nature, and I couldn't help but notice that some of the customers called her Ian, at which she would bow and blow a big, wet kiss. I was just processing all of this when a bloke at my table introduced himself.

"How ya doing mate?" this from a young guy wearing patched Levis and a brown and yellow striped guernsey, "Looking for work?" I didn't have time to reply before he added, "I'm Steve," and offered me a handshake.

"Hi," I replied, deliberately not giving him my name.

I could tell immediately from his accent that he was a Pom, and the recognition was mutual. He was a good talker and, having nothing better to do, I was a good listener. He'd just spent time further north and was running low on cash and, like so many others in town, was hoping to pick up work; if not today, then tomorrow for sure.

"Are you staying for long? I'm kipping at the bunk house round the corner. It's not a palace, but it's cheap."

I quickly weighed up the pros and cons. From what Steve had told me there was plenty of casual labour here, and nobody asked too many questions about identification or work permits. I'd also found a new mate and I reckoned that I would be as safe here as anywhere. So that's how, a few minutes later, I found myself checking out the Mount Isa hostel. The place was almost completely deserted, even though most beds were booked. Everyone was out working at the mines, or at the smelter, or at something to do with both. I decided to grab my car, bring it round and sign in. I was already beginning to figure that the longer I stayed here, the safer I would be.

It took me about five minutes to walk to the car, but on the way back to the hostel I missed a turn and ended up at the back of some marshalling yards and, for a few minutes, got completely lost. By the time I found my bearings and got back to the hostel it was about quarter of an hour later and Steve was waiting for me, sitting on the front steps in the shade.

Before I could get out of the car Steve quickly came over. "Just stay there a minute. There's a guy inside and he's looking for a Pom who sounds suspiciously like you. He's crawling all over town and has been to the café and loads of other places. I got the distinct impression that he wants to see you rather more than you want to see him."

On the back seat, Brutus seemed to be following every word. He tensed, and I thought for one awful moment that he was going to start barking but then, miraculously, he simply yawned, licked his chops and lay panting on the warm leather upholstery.

Steve disappeared and I hunkered down in the driver's seat, making myself as small as possible. I adjusted the rearview mirror and kept an eye on the door of the hostel. A few moments later, Steve emerged. He was talking to someone, and they were both headed my way. From what I could gather, the conversation wasn't going well for either of them, and by now they were closer still. I squeezed down, as far out of sight as possible, and could hear the scrunch of leather soles on gravel as the stranger came closer. I held my breath and prayed that Brutus would stay quiet.

I heard a match being struck, and then smelt the aroma of tobacco. Everything was quiet and the quiet went on for an age. Then I heard a cigarette stub being ground out by a shoe, the sound of a key in a car door, the door opening, the turning of the ignition, the roar of an engine and a car rolling away.

I lay still, not daring to move. And then there was a tap on the window.

I wound it down.

"Christ, what's that smell?"

"It's Brutus," I lied. "He's got a dietary problem."

"Well, I guess you and Brutus need to get out of here and quick. I reckon your mate will be back soon and, if I were you, I wouldn't want to be around."

I thanked Steve, wound down all my windows and hit the road. I reckoned that, with luck, I'd have a good head start before anyone came after me again.

Chapter 28:
We of the never never

The velvet night was silent as we pulled off the Stuart highway. Brutus needed a break, and so did I.

I killed the engine, doused the lights and rolled off the bitumen on to the soft shoulder. I sat for a moment in the silence. Brutus whined softly. The engine clicked gently as it began to cool down. I quietly opened the door, and we stepped out into the desert air.

Above us, the foam of the Milky Way was singing its silent, timeless song to the stars sprinkled like diamonds across a cloudless sky. In the warm night the road ran north, as straight as an arrow. Everything was at peace. For a few minutes I was lost in a reverie, a dreamlike respite from the fear and the hunted feeling of the past days.

In the distance I heard a rumble, then I saw the lights. Too many lights for a car, so I knew it must be a road train, two hundred tons of steel hurling itself towards us. From a distance of maybe half a mile I could feel the road vibrate, and hear the tyres humming on its smooth, black surface, accompanying the throb of its thousand horsepower diesel engine. On it came and then, with an almighty rattling roar and a deafening blast on the air horn, the juggernaut thundered past bound, I guess, for Darwin.

As the taillights disappeared I wondered about having a kip, but thought better of it. This stretch of road was far too exposed, and we might be spotted. Wearily we climbed into the car. I fired the engine and headed back onto the highway.

As the dawn light was creeping over the horizon I pulled off the road by a sign which read *Mataranka Hot Springs*. Hot springs, that was the last thing I wanted, or so I thought. What I needed was somewhere to kip in the shade, out of sight of folks and out of minds, and this place looked as though it would do nicely.

I drove about half a mile down the track, parked in a sandy depression beneath a stand of gum trees and tried to get some shut-eye, but whether it was because of the heat or the adrenaline pumping through my veins, I just couldn't relax. After a short while, in an effort to soothe my nerves, I started talking to myself.

I'm in a big country, right?

Yeah.

So, it's unlikely, I'll be found, right?

Yeah.

So, I'm reasonably safe here, right?

Yeah.

So, I should chill, right?

Yeah.

But I can't.

Yeah. But you already know that.

I needed to calm myself, so I decided to take a walk through the bush. Maybe that would do the trick. Brutus padded silently behind. After about twenty minutes I came to what I presumed were the hot springs, crystal clear and gently steaming. Without thinking I fell forwards into the water and let myself be carried downstream by its warm caress while the air above me was alive with insect life.

I floated into a shallow spot and, in the dappled sunlight, closed my eyes and almost fell into a doze before I hauled myself on to the bank, lay down and sank into a blessed slumber.

Almost immediately I began to dream a vivid dream in which I was running in the Olympic marathon and somehow I was out in front. There was only one other person in the race, and he was catching up on me. I was eyeballs out but it was no good, my lead was being whittled away. I couldn't see my pursuer, but I knew he was there. I kept glancing behind me, but all I could see was an empty road. Even so, I sensed that he was coming, relentlessly like an unstoppable road train. Then, in my dream, I heard him asking questions, searching ceaselessly.

Brutus nuzzled me and I woke in fright, my senses on full alert. I could hear two voices above the gentle murmur of the water. Male voices. I strained to hear what was being said, but I couldn't. Someone, it seemed, was looking for something, or perhaps they were looking for someone. I began to panic. Maybe it was just a family out for a picnic enjoying the day, but maybe it wasn't.

I signalled to Brutus to follow, and we ran quietly back towards the car. Behind us I heard an engine kick into life. I grabbed Brutus and dived out of sight behind a weatherbeaten sign board. A vehicle hurtled past, boiling up a cloud of dust. I couldn't get a glimpse of the driver, but he certainly seemed in a hurry. I was getting a bad feeling in my stomach and wondered whether the driver was alone or if he had company. I wasn't sure what he was looking for, but I had an awful feeling that it might be me.

As Brutus and I emerged from our hiding place, I couldn't help but read the inscription on the signboard. It said simply:

We of the never never

'We of the never never' is a memoir written by Jeannie Gunn, who in 1902 accompanied her husband, Aeneas, from Melbourne, Australia, to this part of the Northern Territory.

The term "Never never" had different connotations to different people. Some people spoke of this land as a place that people would never, never want to go. Others spoke of it as a place people never, never wanted to leave.'

Brutus looked up at me. He seemed to understand. At that moment this was a place I certainly wanted to leave and never, never wanted to come back to.

I also made my mind up. I was tired of hiding in the shadows, always looking over my shoulder, suspecting every single person I met. This was no way to live. Sure, I was scared, but I guess that at that moment I must have been clean out of adrenaline and had no more stomach for running away.

By the time the car had bounced back onto the blacktop of the highway I felt calmer; I had decided to find somewhere quiet and try to live for a while like a normal human being.

"Better to go out in a blaze of glory eh, Brutus?"

Brutus just licked his chops as if to say, que sera, sera.

"Yeah, you are right mate, que sera, sera."

Chapter 29:
Rum Jungle

The road seemed never ending and the air was dancing in the mid-afternoon heat; even with all the windows down I felt as though I was melting. I decided to pull off at the next turning, which seemed to take an age to reach. As I did so, I passed a green and white sign bearing the legend: *Welcome to Rum Jungle. Pop 84.*

As I left the highway I was surprised to see a hoarding advertising scuba diving, wind surfing and canoeing and, sure enough, within a few minutes the road skirted a large lake. It was beautiful, surrounded by verdant bushland. The water was calling me to me to cool off and Brutus was looking a bit done, so I decided to take a plunge.

I rolled onto a gravel patch at the head of a beach, ripped my T-shirt off, discarded my shoes, ran to the edge and threw myself in. The water was dark and refreshing. I took a breath and dived down into the cold depths, while the sunlight skittered above me. I rose and ploughed the surface for a few minutes before lapping lazily to the shore where a family of four was busy manhandling a couple of yellow lilos into the water. If this was life in the north, then it looked just fine by me.

I lay on my towel, dried off and dozed for a while. All my cares were soothed by the warmth of the sun and that glow you get when you have just had a cool swim. I was eventually bought back to reality by the screams and yells of a water fight from the kids on their air beds.

I lay there a short while longer, not wanting to move, but eventually I put on my T-shirt and made my way back to the car. As I did, I saw a metal sign rusting on a tree:

MINE TAILINGS URANIUM-238 KEEP OUT
Danger, elevated gamma radiation, alpha radioactive dust, and significant radon concentrations. Injurious to life.

Despite the heat I shivered and thought about yelling a warning to the folks frolicking in the toxic waste, but from their local registration plates I figured that this wouldn't be news to them, and anyway, I didn't want to rain on their parade.

Rum Jungle town centre consisted of about four features: a telephone booth, a grocery store, an enormous gum tree and what looked to me like the world's biggest pub, the Rum Jungle Hotel.

Now, I have to tell you that its use of the word 'hotel' is probably a crime against advertising standards, it did in fact have rooms, but its main business was beer. As I was checking in, however, I noticed something in its favour, a collection of secondhand paperbacks for guests to borrow. I was looking through them when the receptionist, a young woman, asked if I was looking for anything in particular.

"Oh, I don't know, anything, adventure, foreign travel, stuff like that." One book in particular, looked appealing: *Heart of Darkness*. I picked it up and was scanning it when the receptionist said, "I don't think that's quite what you think it is."

"Why not?"

"Well, the guy who left it here said," and she looked around before whispering quietly, "it's all about a bloke who takes a steamer up the Congo, if you know what I mean."

Nevertheless I took it, and the key to a room that looked and felt as though it had been made of a combination of wood chip and asbestos fibre. Its saving grace was the fact that it had both a shower that actually worked and a functioning air con unit. I showered, put food out on the verandah for Brutus and lay on the bed with my book, but had only read a couple of pages before I dozed off.

I woke about half an hour later, checked on Brutus and went in search of food.

I guess you've heard of Phil Spector's famous 'wall of sound'. Well, entering the bar, the effect was as if someone had turned up all the faders to get full saturation. I reckoned that whoever had come up with the town's population figure on its road sign had had omitted to count the folks at the pub.

It took a couple of moments to recover from the wave of noise and for my eyes to adjust as I stepped into the maelstrom. The place was heaving with what must have been over a hundred blokes, all wearing blue stubbies and stained singlets, chugging down beers as though there was no tomorrow, which, judging from the signs by the lake, might have been a wise precaution.

The 'counter tea' was in full swing. The idea was just front up, place your order, get a ticket and wait for your number to be called. This seemed like a foolproof system but, what with all the drinking, there were a few mishaps. Shortly after I had got my tucker a brawl erupted over something called a 'four and twenty pie and chips'. Apparently, someone somewhere in the supply and demand chain had got their wires crossed and the right food had ended up with the wrong bloke – if you catch my drift.

I had opted for the barramundi which, hereafter, I will refer to as the hot water bottle fish, so named because it was deep fried with about an inch of batter on its outside covering an object that looked like a fillet of fish but had the taste and consistency of rubber. I was just wondering if what I was eating had formerly inhabited the local swimming hole when the waitress rolled up.

"Aren'tcha eating that?" I smiled in a way that was meant to say 'maybe' as I didn't want to hurt her feelings. I needn't have bothered, because she barked, "Well get a flaming shift on you mongrel. There's plenty of folks waiting for your plate."

I didn't finish the fish. I might have done had I had a Geiger counter, but the more I looked at it, the more worried I became. Eventually I stood up, walked towards a serving hatch and levered the remains into a large plastic dustbin which was almost overflowing with uneaten food. As the fish slipped off my plate I remember feeling thankful that that was one meal that I'd never see again. Unfortunately, however, I was mistaken.

I was minding my own business when a bloke joined me at the table. He was carrying a very large jug of beer and three glasses.

"I'm Wiry Tony."

"G'day, I'm Jack." Quite why I had used the name Jack when I checked in is still a puzzle, but there it was, and I was stuck with it.

"You're not that flaming hit man are you?" Wiry Tony laughed and jerked his thumb towards the TV screen which was showing a photofit of someone who bore a passing resemblance to a Picasso painting – you know the sort, where the subject looks like a cross between a horse and a human, and more than likely has an ear in the wrong place.

Before I could respond Tony laughed and grunted "Howdya fancy some action?"

I was relieved that my resemblance to the fugitive was meant as a joke, but Tony's question put me in a bit of a quandary. Was he asking if I was looking for some action with him? And if so, what sort of action? I was already worried that, interested or not, I might not have much choice in the matter. Just then, out of the corner of my eye, I saw the waitress making her way over to us. She was the only woman in the place and seemed especially interested in our conversation. Surely, I wasn't being offered some kind of outback silver service, was I?

Wiry Tony leant in towards me. "Have you ever tried two up?"

My mind was racing, I was having a waking nightmare. I didn't know what a 'two up' was, but it clearly involved me and both of my new chums.

The waitress parked herself next to me. "Hi, I'm Raelene, Tony has something he'd like to share with you." I mentally reeled.

Tony put his hand down the front of his stubbies, while I feared the worst. He leant forward, grabbed my arm and said, "Cop a look at this."

I hardly dared look. When I did, I was both surprised and relieved. There on the table was a flat piece of wood about a foot long. Sitting alongside it were two old pennies.

Raelene continued, "This is the kip. Tony's the ringer. He runs the shoot. He picks a spinner who chucks the coins into the air and folks bet on the outcome – two heads, two tails or one of each. It's a big thing. It's illegal but no one gives a rat's arse at a wedding. Sid, in the corner," she nodded to a guy drinking by himself, "he's the boxer. He's here to sort out any trouble."

"What's in it for me?"

"Plenty." Raelene smiled, and handed me two coins. They looked identical to the ones Tony had. "Just look after these beauties and when Tony tips you the wink you'll be the spinner. All you have to do is the switch and just make sure that when you throw them, the coins spin, otherwise you're screwed."

I smiled. I knew that what I was being asked to do was part of some sort of scam, but I only had about fifty dollars left, so even if the worst came to the worst I couldn't really be much worse off, could I?

The two up game was held in the back yard of the hotel. Wiry

Tony had already drummed up a fair few customers.

I watched and found it all a bit confusing. Blokes would tap their heads with piles of cash. These were betting that both coins landed on heads. They quickly paired off with individuals backing tails. The game seemed simple and foolproof. After a slow start, things began to warm up. About two thirds of the pub was now involved, either betting or simply watching.

The spinner was passed from hand to hand, the coins rose and fell, and money was exchanged. I was getting really engrossed when, after about twenty minutes, I got jostled and felt a shove in my back. When I reached into my pockets the two pennies were gone. Almost immediately Wiry Tony shot me a glance.

Time stood still, the kip was pressed into my hand. I wanted to yell to Tony that the scam was off, but I couldn't. As I held the kip, I scanned the crowd. The waitress was waving a large number of notes at her head. I was in a bind. I had blown the plan, but I couldn't back out. I flipped the coins, they rose into the air and fell together in the dirt.

"HEADS." A roar went up. Both coins had landed with the King's face uppermost.

I was sweating. Somehow, I had gotten away with it. But the kip was back in my hand. The waitress now had twice as much cash and was waving it about her head and drawing in large numbers of customers.

When all the bets were laid, I flipped the coins again. Time seemed to stand still as the coins rose slowly, revolved and fell back to earth.

"HEADS."

Again, two heads were face up. The odds against this were pretty high, about 16 to 1 I reckon. The chances of it happening three times in a row must be about 50 to 1. The crowd knew this and bets were flying in towards the waitress who had an enormous pile of cash and was tapping her head vigorously.

My hands were sweating as I raised the kip. I realised that the fix was for consecutive heads to pay out, the only problem was that I had no control over the outcome. The coins soared once again, higher than before and came down together in the dirt. I couldn't look but I didn't have to, the roar from the crowd told me.

"HEADS."

To one side I could see Raelene moving out of the crowd and then Wiry Tony was taking the kip from me and handing it on.

Back in the bar, the TV screen was broadcasting a re-run of an Aussie Rules game to an almost empty gallery. It was unnaturally calm after the mayhem in the back yard. Raelene was looking mighty pleased and, as I ordered a beer, she nodded to the bartender. "Here's Jack, he's a friend, whatever he wants, it's on me." As she passed by, she slipped me something, a roll of fifty dollar banknotes wrapped in a jumbo elastic band.

"Seems like your luck's in mate." This from an incredibly ugly old timer with one eye. "I don't know how you pulled that one, but you sure had me going." I shot a puzzled glance. My new acquaintance smiled and slid something across the bar to me, the two pennies I had lost earlier. "I lifted these from you before you got the kip. Now tell me Jack, if that really is your name, how did you do it?"

I smiled. When in doubt, tell the truth is my rule of thumb. So, without looking up I told it, plain, simple and unvarnished.

"Beginner's luck." I smiled and sculled my beer.

One-eye thumped me on the back and, although he laughed, I could tell that he was unhappy with my answer, nevertheless he yelled to the barman, "Two more beers mate, and an extra one for me new chum while you're about it."

What I didn't realise at the time was that One-eye had lifted something else, my wallet. Had I known, it wouldn't have worried me too much. After all I had a roll of notes in my pocket and there wasn't much in the wallet apart from a few receipts. Little could I know that its loss was going to put me in danger once again.

Towards the end of the night I saw Wiry Tony once more. He was in fine form, dancing with a life-sized blow-up model of a saltwater crocodile which had been conjured up from God knows where. He was heading out with a few mates to the lake and invited me to join them and that is how, a while later, I found myself, Brutus in tow, back on the beach that I'd visited earlier that day.

A few of the blokes had stripped off and were half swimming, half drowning in the tropic night air, and I probably would have joined them had there not been a rather violent chemical reaction between the hot water bottle fish and the beer I'd been drinking. I vaguely remember coming face to face once more with the barramundi as it struggled successfully to regain its former habitat.

For the second time in less than twenty-four hours I fell asleep by the lake, and this time I didn't wake up for several hours.

Back at the hotel, a new guest had checked in, someone clearly out of place, dressed in a dark Italian suit. Although it was late, he was mingling at the bar, keen to find out about other customers, especially anyone who might be called Jack. Sometime later, or so I heard, he was seen in deep conversation with the bloke with one eye and apparently at one point in the proceedings the suited man stood up and was heard to mutter, "Good on yer. Let's go and find him."

The two of them left. I didn't know it, but the mob was closing in on me.

Chapter 30:
That's all for now, Jack

I woke with a shiver. An early morning breeze was riffling the surface of the lake. Brutus was lying by my side, sleeping the sleep of the just.

My shirt was matted with the remains of last night's counter tea and my mouth felt as though it was full of sawdust.

I stretched and yawned. Lying nearby were a number of other bodies, survivors from last night's goings on at the Rum Jungle Hotel.

I got up unsteadily to my feet, shucked off my shoes and clothes and made my way to the water's edge. I shivered slightly as I waded in, and then kicked off for a wooden swimming platform that was anchored about fifty metres offshore.

As I swam, my blood seemed to fizz and pop and I felt life returning to my body.

I hauled myself onto the platform and lay down, letting the rising sun warm my body and leach out the toxins from last night's overindulgence. The early morning air warmed up quickly and, in a few moments, my eyes closed and I dozed off again.

I'm not sure how much later it was that I woke up, but it couldn't have been long. I think it must have been the sound of Brutus. I lazily lifted an eye and looked towards the beach. I could see Brutus lying prone; standing above him were two men, one brandishing a tyre iron. Brutus stirred and began to rise but as he did, he received a terrible blow to his head, let out a low moan and lay still.

I felt a wave of anger rise up in me, but I felt powerless. I recognised the bloke with the weapon, it was One-eye, but the other was a mystery to me. One of them, I think the guy in the suit, kicked Brutus a couple of times, but Brutus did not move.

The new arrivals then began rousing some of the other revellers and, although I couldn't hear clearly what was being said, the drift of the voices told me that they were looking for someone, and that someone was me.

I'd been lucky so far, they hadn't spotted me. I began to weigh up my options. If I stayed here, they were sure to find me. Even if I tried to swim for it, they surely would see me. While I was searching for options, I lay perfectly still watching them closely. The man in the suit was scanning everywhere. Eventually, of course, his eyes rested on the swimming platform. Our eyes met and it was almost as though we could read each other's minds. He was here to kill me, and I was terrified. My legs began to shake, and the taste of the hot water bottle fish rose up again in my throat. I was watching his every move. What happened next surprised me, but perhaps it shouldn't have. He walked to the back of the beach. I waited. He returned moments later carrying something in his arms. A rifle. I watched transfixed as he loaded it and checked the telescopic sight before raising it and drawing a bead on me.

I pushed myself backwards off the far side of the swimming platform. As my head went under the water I heard a 'clump' and saw a silver trail streak through the water, leaving behind fragments where the bullet had hit the wooden planking.

Seconds later, another streak passed my left shoulder. And then another just in front of my face. The gunman was shooting blind, but I was running out of breath and I knew that as soon as my head popped up, I'd be toast.

I had no choice, my lungs were burning, so I did the only thing possible, I resurfaced underneath the platform. There was space under there, maybe a foot or so, enough to breathe. The gunman however had anticipated this, and three rapid shots clumped through the wooden boards close to my head.

I took a deep breath, dived deep and headed towards a rocky headland I'd seen, about seventy-five yards away. It was surrounded by thick bush, and this seemed to be my best and only means of escape.

As I swam, part of my mind wanted me to surface and to get this terror over with as quickly as possible, but another part of me simply wanted to survive and I guess that was the part that won the argument.

Swimming seventy-five yards underwater is not the sort of thing most people do most days. I reckon it must have taken me almost two minutes before I saw the lake bed begin to shelve upwards. Above me I could see bright sunlight and knew that I had to wait until I reached the shade of the overhanging bush before there was the remotest chance of getting out without being seen. I forced myself to carry on. Ten more yards and still the sky was bright above and then, on the edge of hope, I encountered some rocks, and, as I rounded them, I entered a shadowed area and judged that it was safe to emerge. As my head broke the surface I saw that I was in a small bay surrounded by dense vegetation. A little hope began to spring inside me and I thought that, with a bit of luck, I just might escape with my life. There was no time to lose, however. I had to get out of the water fast and find a place to lie low.

As I got unsteadily to my feet, I heard the unmistakable sound of a rifle being cocked and looked up to see the barrel of a gun no more than three feet from my face.

One-eye stood next to his new mate, bloodied tyre lever in hand. The suit spoke.

"Well Jack, you're a hard man to track down. But I guess this is the end of the highway. We can do this quick and easy or take our time. The quick way, is a bullet, the alternative… Well, I'll leave that to your imagination." I didn't care. I was angry, I was going to die anyway.

The suit looked at me. "Where is it, the dope you stole from down south?"

I laughed. " Why don't you ask your mate?" I nodded towards One eye, " I sold it to him."

One-eye wasn't expecting this. As I said, I didn't care, I was going to have his arse for what he'd done to Brutus. He looked as though he'd just won first prize in the all the kangaroo testicles you can eat competition. The colour drained from his face.

"That's a lie, he's just saying that to save his neck."

The suit was weighing this up. "Maybe, maybe not." He swivelled and put a bullet straight through One-eye's foot and then put the muzzle to his forehead."One chance mate, have you got the dope?"

Through the pain, One-eye managed to croak, "No, I told you…"

I will never know how that sentence would have ended. The suit calmly and deliberately shot him in the face.

He turned and looked at me. "Seems like you must've been lying." He pointed with his thumb at the wreckage of One-eye. "He'd have told me if he could. I'm gonna count to three and then I want an answer."

I laughed. "OK, I'll tell you. I smoked it, all one thousand kilos. Mind you it tasted like shit."

The suit was not amused.

He pointed the gun at me and, as I waited for the end, the world exploded into a whirl of boiling flesh, blood, intestines and the finest Italian silk.

Brutus was in a frenzy. He tore at my assailant with a biblical ferocity, and then for good measure tore even more. Just when I thought things couldn't get much uglier I saw I was wrong. Brutus went into a fury of snapping, dragging, tearing, ripping and pulling.

When I thought he had finished he turned to the remains of One-eye and drove his jaws deep into his chest cavity. Brutus was possessed. His face was smeared with gore and he began throwing his head from side to side and each time he did so a chunk of something horrible detached itself from the body and sailed into the undergrowth.

I sat down shaking, and called repeatedly to Brutus to calm down. I didn't think it would work but, the third time, he slowed, then stopped and loped over towards me and lay at my feet breathing heavily. He gave me a look which seemed to say, 'sorry, I shouldn't have done that'. I burst into tears, and for the first time I gave him a hug. When I did this, the strangest thing happened. Brutus lay down, closed his eyes and his tail began whirring like the blades on a helicopter.

In the meantime, someone from the beach had called the cops and when they turned up a few minutes later with the meat waggon they had plenty of questions.

I'm a bit confused about what happened next. Apparently, Wiry Tony took charge. He had seen it all clearly. The two blokes who had gone for the long ride had been standing at the water's edge when they were taken by an enormous crocodile. Tony couldn't be sure, but he said he thought it was Salty Joe, a creature of legend. The locals said that they thought that he had died years ago at the height of the mining boom, but Tony told the police that, to be honest, he was never convinced.

I wasn't sure the police would swallow this tale, but after a brief look at the bodies and one of the officers vomiting into a bush, they issued instructions that crocodile warnings were to be posted all around the lake.

After things quietened down Wiry Tony drove me and Brutus back to the hotel.

"Listen mate, whatever is going on, your secret's safe with the folks out here. I don't know about you, but that bloke in the suit scared the bejesus out of everyone. In any case, half the folks here are hiding from something or another and I can't imagine many want to get involved with the police. If I were you, I'd lie low for a couple of weeks in the eye of the storm. If anyone is still looking for you, I reckon that this is the last place they'll expect you to be."

As it happens, no one did come looking for me, probably on account of a strange twist of fate. Whilst examining the bodies, a detective who'd been hauled in from Darwin found a wallet on one of the bodies, which contained one particular item which grabbed their attention.

Jolly Swagman Caravan and Camping site

Rockhampton

QLD

Vehicle Reg/ Make	VFC 484		Valiant
Title	Family name	Forename	
Mr	Nicholson	Jack	
Arrival Date	Departure date	Van no	Van rate
01/04/84	02/04/84	4	14.00

On the other victim was a driving licence. In record time the police put two and two together and came up with five.

• • •

The *Territorial* newspaper led with the banner headline:
Nicholson Jacks in his chips,
and the subtitle:
Sunshine Sam sleeps with the fishes.
Two bodies found at a lake outside the township of Rum Jungle have been identified as Sam Gioconda and Jack Nicholson. Both are understood to have underworld connections. Mr. Gioconda is known to gangland associate as 'Sunshine Sam' and is understood to have had business dealings with Mr. Nicholson, who has been linked to at least two gangland hits in the past month, including those of Maurizio Scarabelli and 'Lucky' Lenny Landolpho. He is also thought to be the so called 'Silo Killer'.

The report concluded with a statement from the police stressing the importance of the photofit likeness of Mr. Nicholson.

"Not only was the image an almost perfect match but the victim was in possession of a number of items, including a wallet which confirmed his identity. As far as we are concerned the investigation into Mr. Nicholson is closed."

Local TV stations were full of the story which seemed to be on an almost endless repeat cycle. As I watched, a blonde reporter was standing by the lake filing her report.

"The pair appear to have been attacked by a large saltwater crocodile in an area that, for years, has been assumed to be perfectly safe. A local wildlife expert, Tony Wilson, says a seven metre saltwater crocodile has been seen regularly in the area in recent weeks." The camera then panned to the 'expert witness'. It was Wiry Tony, who then gave a vivid description of the attack.

The next camera shot was of a newly erected sign, black on a yellow background, sporting an image of an open mouthed maneater.

DANGER
Crocodiles inhabit this area. Attacks cause injury or death.
Do not enter the water.
Do not clean fish near the water's edge.
Remove all food and fish waste.

I was a bit worried that this might ruin days out at the lake but Tony later informed me that the signs would make no difference as everyone in town knew that the story was, as he put it, "A real crock."

Chapter 31:
The Kurdaitcha man

The Kurdaitcha man is a ritual executioner **Australian Aboriginal** *culture. Among traditional Indigenous Australians there is no such thing as a belief in natural death. All deaths are considered to be the result of evil spirits or spells, usually influenced by an enemy. Often, a dying person will whisper the name of the person they think caused their death. If the identity of the guilty person is not known, a "magic man" will watch for a sign, such as an animal burrow leading from the grave showing the direction of the home of the guilty party. This may take years but the identity is always eventually discovered. The elders of the mob that the deceased belonged to then hold a meeting to decide a suitable punishment. A Kurdaitcha may or may not be arranged to avenge them. The practice of Kurdaitcha had died out completely in southern Australia by the twentieth century although it was still carried out infrequently in the north. The practice, in regard to bone pointing by itself, does continue into modern times albeit very rarely.*

The name Kurdaitcha is also used by Europeans to refer to the oval shoes worn by the Kurdaitcha. The shoe is basically a mat of feathers mixed with human blood in such a way that the blood cannot be detected and even a close examination does not reveal how the feathers remain stuck together. The upper surface is covered with a net woven from human hair. An opening in the centre allows the foot to be inserted. When in use, they are decorated with lines of white and pink **down** *and are said to leave no tracks.*

Source: Wikipedia

I think of him as the Kurdaitcha man and even now I'm not sure why.

It was late afternoon when I saw him, just standing there on the empty road at the edge of the vast Barclay Downs.

How he got to that empty stretch is anyone's guess, but he was clearly expecting someone, and that someone was me. I hadn't seen a car for almost an hour, but shortly before he appeared Brutus did something very strange. He whimpered, jumped up from the front seat and scrambled into the back as if clearing a space for someone.

I didn't really have a choice about stopping, it was as though something, or someone, else was in control of my actions. The tyres scrunched the gravel as the car slewed to a halt. The man opened the door and climbed in. I knew even before I stopped who he was - the quiet man from the Wellshot Hotel.

As I drove, we talked, though we didn't say a word. He let me know about his tribe, his flesh and his animal totem. His mind was asking, "What is your flesh?" and I tried as best as I could to explain my tribal roots. My vagueness seemed to disappoint and surprise him. Without uttering a word, he told me that he knew that I shared his totemic animal. He knew this because he had seen me save his totem in a dream. My mind went back to that day, a lifetime ago, by the abandoned well and the lizard I had rescued.

My friend smiled. All things are connected in the dreamtime, he told me. People, places, plants, animals, the past, the present and the future. I understood that, if I wanted, I could become one with the dreaming.

I'm not sure how long our conversation lasted, but it must have been several hours because the sun was reddening the western sky as we entered a wide expanse of emptiness about an hour east of the small township of Boulia.

I pulled up off the road by a small stand of eucalypts, threw my swag on the ground and lit a fire. My friend filled the billy and we watched it boil while the stars above turned through their gears slowly in the night sky.

As the temperature plummeted, erratic lights appeared along the curve of the horizon. My companion let me know that these were the fabled Min Min lights, which have existed in this part of the outback for as long as time itself. We watched as they moved, changing from white to red and green, disappearing, approaching and then receding, all the while dancing to a silent tune.

While we watched my friend had a secret that he offered to share. I can't really explain it, but I'll have a go. The world, he explained, was not quite as I saw it. There were other ways of seeing, but to use them required great courage.

"Once you see the other side you can never quite go back," he told me. "You will be forever between two ways of seeing but you already know some of that, because you see that in me."

And so there it was. A choice was being given to me; a door into the great unknown, but it was a one way door. Was I going to step through it?

The fact that I'm writing this tells you that I didn't. I just did not feel prepared, and that felt perfectly okay. Finally, I began to feel weary and lay down on my swag and watched the sparks from the fire rise lazily into the night.

Grey light was seeping through the trees when I awoke. The lights had disappeared. Brutus was lying by my side but my friend had gone, slipping away like a ghost in the night. In fact, I almost began to wonder whether all of the previous day had merely been a dream.

After a brew and a bite to eat I loaded the car and was about to set off when I noticed something on the dashboard, an oval piece of carved pearl shell, a hole in one end through which a cord was passed. Its surface was covered in a series of whorls painted in a brown pigment, but as I looked at it other shapes began to emerge, in particular, an object that looked like a seed, a bindi eye. On the reverse was a creature, a lizard, staring at me across the years from the day it was created. I held the object for a few minutes, then gently picked it up and hung it around my neck and, as I did so, I felt a sense of peace and connection with the world.

Chapter 32:
Return of the native

The flatlands north of Rainbow are bathed in the warm light of late afternoon. Brutus has given up tearing the upholstery to pieces and is dozing on the back seat.

I'm feeling tired and looking forward to getting back to normal, after all it has been an emotional ride.

A short while after leaving Nhill, I catch sight of the grain silos. They look different today, welcoming and familiar. Somehow I sense that they are guiding me home.

It's as though time is repeating itself, and after a few minutes I'm pulling up alongside Bill's caravan. I hit the iron gate with the piece of steel that doubles for the doorknocker but there is no response, even the dogs are missing. Further on, Matthew's Farm Supplies is similarly quiet, and I begin to get an uneasy feeling. When I reach Federal Street it is as though I'm on the film set of *On the Beach* – you know the scene, the one where, after the nuclear war, Melbourne is absolutely devoid of people. Even the High School and the Eureka Hotel are closed.

I try the door of Stan's general store and find it locked, but posted in the window there is a notice.

CLOSED WEDNESDAY AFTERNOON. TOMMO'S MEMORIAL.

And underneath another piece of card.

LEATHER BRACES $1.00 PER PAIR. TWO PAIRS FOR $1.50.
I pick up a copy of the Jeparit Bugle from the paper rack.

There it is, on the front page in the bottom left hand corner, a small article advertising the memorial service and summarising the disappearance and presumed death of Rainbow's shortest serving secondary school teacher. Underneath is a story about Mario, *Savage Beating of Local Shopkeeper*.

I make my way along Federal Street towards the railway line and head north. I had forgotten how hot this place can be. Brutus is padding along behind me, panting noisily, tongue lolling. Up ahead cars are baking in the afternoon sun, clustered around the Lutheran church from which I can hear the strains of *Up There Cazaly* being sung by what I imagine must be the world's worst Aussie rules football choir. The service is apparently quite an event and, in anticipation of media interest, a couple of speakers have been wired up and are beaming the service to a bored looking bunch of reporters sitting in the shade outside, shooting the breeze and cracking cans of Victoria Bitter. Judging from the pile of empties it looks as though they have been there for a while. As the singing dies down, I hear the unmistakable voice of Bill Harding.

"That was Tommo's favourite song and I know it's hardly the sort of thing that you might have expected to hear on a day like today. Although he was only here for a short while, because of his love of footy, me and the lads think that somehow he would have rather liked it."

The amplification is quite good and I can hear clearly a murmur of assent from the assembled congregation.

The minister is next up. There is an audible shuffling and coughing, and then in sombre tones he begins his sermon.

"Tommo loved the horses and was fond of the odd wager." A murmur of assent rises up. "Well, Tommo's race has been run, and if I know anything, he'll be in that winner's enclosure just inside the pearly gates. He lived his life as if it were the Inter Dominion Handicap, nothing held back, striving to be the best. I know that Tommo wouldn't have wanted money for flowers, so today's collection will be in support of the Disabled Jockeys' Association, a charity that I like to think Tommo would have approved of.

"Let us now sing the next hymn on your song sheet: *Here's a race for us to run*."

The organ pipes up and then the singing bursts from the speaker:

Here's a race for us to run,
And a way for us the race to win.
To all those who have begun,
God has spoken, Look away to Him!

Someone else then begins to intone. I have no idea who this person is, and I think the feeling is mutual. He goes on about the fact that we have one life on earth and then live for eternity in heaven. He talks about sin, redemption, piety and lots of other things that normal people hardly ever talk about. He alludes to all the good things that I apparently did in my life, and I must admit to being rather surprised and impressed by this and even find myself wondering whether I have come to the wrong service.

I'm feeling edgy and rather guilty and wondering how I'm going to announce my return. The tension builds and builds and then something inside me snaps. I tie Brutus to the fence, take a deep breath and, telling myself that this will all be over in a minute, march up to the entrance.

The eulogy is reaching a climax and so no one notices me as I slide in.

"So, what would Tommo say if he were here today?"

This clearly is my Neil Armstrong moment. It is as if a divine being is telling me that I have to say something profound and memorable. It's a never-to-be-repeated chance of immortality and I have to seize it, so I steel myself and, metaphorically speaking, step up to the plate. As if from miles away, I hear myself uttering those immortal words, that, as Jung would have said, emanated from the cosmic unconsciousness. "To hell with the disabled jockeys, who fancies a beer?"

Chapter 33:
The return of the mummy

Down at the Eureka Hotel, things are really humming.

Drinks are pushed into my hand and my back is bruised from so many slaps. Everyone, it seems, wants to know what's happened to me.

I have concocted a tale which I only hope will improve with time. In this version of events I am completely innocent and have been abducted by the guy known as Jack Nicholson. He has tortured me and dumped me down a disused well at a property a few miles out of town. I describe the place Mario and I visited weeks ago, so I reckon I sound convincing. People nod, they know the place. I explain that I was tied up and blindfolded, and because of the blindfold I have no idea how long I was there before I managed to extricate myself. For much of the time, so my story went, I must have been in a semi-conscious state, and, as a result of everything, there are large gaps in my memory which, considering everything that really did happen to me, is quite convenient. I also can't explain where my new mate Brutus came from. As I warm to the tale, making all this up on the hoof, I'm relaxed as I'm pretty sure that any discrepancies will be put down to the fact that most of the audience were pretty plastered and besides, I was in a state of post-traumatic stress, wasn't I?

One person however is missing: Mario. Partway through the evening Allegra comes into the bar and there is a sudden hush. She walks up to me, embraces me, and kisses me on both cheeks. She hands me a giant gift-wrapped cauliflower and whispers in my ear, "Mario, he's in hospital. He wants to see you. Will you come now?"

My heart is singing. I'm both relieved and surprised that he has survived.

I climb up onto the bar and try to say a few words of thanks and goodnight to all of my friends, but by this stage in the evening no one is really listening and the disabled jockeys' fund seems to be draining at a rate of knots. So I make a quiet exit with Allegra and together we drive in silence to the bush hospital in Jeparit.

When we arrive, everything is quiet. There are just one or two lights on. We press the buzzer at the main entrance, and a few seconds later someone comes to open the door. It's Stella. There are tears in her eyes. She seems genuinely pleased to see me in one piece. "Sorry I missed your funeral Tommo but, you know, I've been kind of busy. Mario's through here. Just follow me."

We walk into a small private room. Mario is wired to an array of machines, Both of his legs and one arm are encased in plaster and his head is swathed in bandages. I feel shocked, not just by his appearance, but also by the fact that music is blaring out from a cassette player on his bedside table: his favourite band, The Mentals, singing something about chemicals wiping out brain cells.

Stella shuts the door and draws the curtains.

From the bandaged face a voice emerges, Mario.

"I reckon I'm better at this than Boris Karloff," Mario begins to laugh. Allegra and Stella are also laughing, and I'm puzzled. "I told you I had a plan. Stella fixed it up for me perfectly. The evening you left, Allegra reported an attack on me and Stella whipped me in here and in no time she had enough bandages on me to make me look like a refugee from the reign of Ramses the Third. I hoped that that would throw the mob, and it looks like it did. I guess they figured out that somebody else was involved in the dope heist, and when that character Jack Nicholson appeared on the scene it clinched the deal, so it looks as though we are in the clear. The only thing I can't figure out is just who was Jack Nicholson."

I smiled. I was thinking about Mario's inability to keep a secret so I just said, "It's a long story and perhaps it's best you never know."

There was quiet for a moment and then Stella chipped in.

"Just so you know, as far as everyone in town is aware, Mario is undergoing intensive rehabilitation. We are announcing tomorrow that he has just recovered consciousness. Over the next few weeks we're going to progressively remove the bandages and plasters. In my professional opinion he's going to make a complete recovery." She smiled.

For some reason I was crying, partly through humour, but it was mainly relief. Stella put her arms around me and kissed me on the cheek.

"It's okay, it's all going to be okay."

For the first time in a long while I had the feeling that I was no longer running away from something and that maybe, just possibly, there was something, or someone, that I should run towards.

In the background the tape was still running. It had moved to another track.

"Come up to my place and live it up."

Stella hugged me and then kissed me again, but this time it wasn't on the cheek.

Chapter 34:
Miracle on Charles Street

The Jeparit Bugle had a record week of sales : first there was the news of my reappearance, following hot on its heels was the miraculous recovery of Mario at the bush hospital. According to the story I had taken in some of his favourite music and, when it kicked in, Mario had managed to open one eye.

Greg Pritchard covered the story.

Bush nurse Stella Simpson said yesterday, 'Mario is not yet out of the woods, but is managing to communicate using hand signals. From what we can tell he has no recollection of who or what caused his injuries. We are hopeful that, given time, he will eventually make a good physical recovery, although the psychological scars may take much longer to heal. Tommo is also being cared for by us. As you may imagine, following his ordeal he is in a fragile mental state. Nevertheless, he has agreed to talk briefly to the press.'

The press conference took place in the lounge bar of the Hindmarsh Hotel where, with Stella by my side, I went through an imaginative account of my abduction and battle for survival. The fact that I had been supposedly chucked down a well wasn't enough for the reporters however, who took great liberties with the story. Channel 9 News led their evening bulletin with a feature entitled *Buried alive in the outback*, while ABC news were only a little more circumspect, *Left for dead in the desert*. Both had stories of my incredible bravery. Experts were brought in to explain that I had only survived by a stroke of good luck, the thunderstorm which had dumped half an inch of rain on the night of my disappearance must have enabled me to drink from puddles in the base of the well.

The story was hot for a short while, a typical nine-day wonder and, as interest started to wane, I began to get ready to move on. In a strange way I was becoming attached to the place, and the longer I stayed, the stronger the attachment grew. This gave me a feeling of unease, and I realised that if I didn't leave soon, then perhaps I never would. The clincher was the fact that the school had drafted in a supply teacher who was keen to stay and, as far as I could tell, was a much better teacher and far less of a health and safety threat to the kids than I was.

I had moved back to my old place in Rainbow and had been given free use of a secondhand Holden, courtesy of Dimboola Motors who arranged a photoshoot which I hope made it worth their while.

Before leaving town, I made a farewell tour. I visited the school, spoke at an assembly and wished everyone good luck. I made a few purchases at the general store where Stan gave me a pair of braces 'to remember us by'. After that, I dropped off at the vegetable store where Allegra was holding the fort.

As we said our goodbyes, a young bloke loaded my car with produce.

"Mario wanted you to have this," Allegra said, pointing at the growing pile of stuff in the boot. She looked into the distance, squeezed my hand and said quietly, "Keep in touch, don't be a stranger."

Noon found me sitting outside the café on Federal Street drinking coffee with Stella. The car was packed with everything I owned. I was not coming back.

Brutus was quiet as we left. For a while now he had been as good as gold. Something had changed within him. Perhaps it was the change of diet, perhaps it was something else. I just don't know. Anyway, there he sat, tongue lolling, seemingly eager to get on the road.

As we rolled out of town, I watched the past receding in my wing mirror. Out past the Eureka Hotel and its video horseracing sessions, past Bill's caravan with the flag at half mast, alongside Lake Hindmarsh, through Jeparit with its statue of Iron Bob Menzies, and then of course the hospital where I bid adieu to Mario.

"You see the boys beat the mongrels?"

"Yeah." I'd read the report in the paper about the famous victory.

We were quiet for a few moments then Mario said, "I'm sorry for everything that happened," and he said this in a way that told me that he meant it.

I was lost for words, and we sat there in silence looking everywhere but at each other.

"Probably won't see you again," I said.

"Not if I see you first."

"Well, we had an adventure, it will be something to tell the grandkids."

We both smiled.

I leant over and gave him a hug.

"Did Allegra give you the veggies?"

"Yeah. Thanks. "

"I told you that if you came with me to Vic market you'd get more than a cauliflower." We laughed and then Mario looked away. It was time to go. As I reached the door Mario signalled to me, he had one more thing on his mind. "Just live it up Tommo."

I smiled, turned and left.

My last pause was at the rabbit-proof fence, where I got out of the car to take a final photograph for old time's sake and, I guess, to prevent the past from disappearing completely.

As I parked and stepped out the heat was again ferocious, but by now it seemed like an old friend, constant and reliable. I had to take the photograph quickly and move on, otherwise I felt I might never get away. This place was getting hold of me and the hold was growing stronger all the time and I was getting a little anxious, especially as my camera seemed to have gone missing. For a few minutes while I searched for it, I felt as if I was in one of those dreams, you know the sort, the ones where no matter what you try you just can't escape. For a while I thought I must have left it behind and was about to head back to Rainbow to look for it when I remembered. It was one of the first things I'd packed, it was in a day pack in the boot and was now buried beneath all the veggies.

I opened the boot and started moving stuff. Allegra and Mario had been more than generous, and it took a few minutes to shift things out of the way. Eventually I found the camera hidden, as it happens, by a large plastic sack bearing the legend *SSP, Single Super Phosphate 25 KG*.

I laughed, grabbed the camera, and framed the picture. In the viewfinder the Mallee stretched away for ever, baking in the heat while mirages danced and swam. I pressed the shutter release, turned away, got back into the car, turned on the radio and drove off in the sunshine.

Across the airwaves came the news that Mellox Worming tablets were on special offer at Elder's store in Dimboola and the weather forecast was fine and dry with a top temperature of 35 degrees.

I put my sunglasses on, turned the air con to full power, put my foot down and headed south.

Chapter 35
Brutus's story part 2

It's odd but ever since we left Norm's place, I've had the strangest feeling that I'm going home.

That late afternoon, as we drove, and the sunshine flickered through the trees and caressed my eyes, the feeling grew stronger.

Tommo is a strange bloke. I don't think he likes dogs very much but I'm sure he isn't going to hurt me. When we got back to Rainbow from up north he kept telling me that we were going somewhere that I would like, and at first, a part of me thought it was some of that 'Happy Farm' bullshit. However, I gradually began to believe him and, as the days went by, this feeling grew stronger. Tommo would talk to me and pat me, and in return, I learned to lie on my back and let him tickle my stomach without trying to bite his hand off.

As we drove into the big city, smells and sights which I had long forgotten came drifting back to me. I imagined that I could hear my mother calling me, "Derek, time for dinner." We left the highway and then my hackles rose. Somewhere near here was a dog pound. I could smell it, fear, loneliness and death. I got really agitated, but Tommo took a hand off of the wheel and stroked my neck. I know that he had no idea what I was thinking, but he knew I was upset and he really reassured me.

As we travelled deeper into the city, more memories came flooding back. I recognised a lamppost, one of my favourites, and then a butcher's shop, and a playground where a bunch of us used to meet and keep the neighbours awake all night with our barking. I began to feel excited and Tommo had to keep telling me to settle down. Finally, the excitement was almost too much to bear. I began singing. I knew Tommo liked singing because he was always groaning along to tunes on the radio, and I guess that he liked my singing because he started laughing and joining in.

Eventually we turned into a small street and parked outside a house which was almost completely hidden by trees and weeds. There was something about this place which seemed familiar even though I'd never been there before. Tommo tapped the horn on the car and a few seconds later someone emerged. Even though I hadn't seen him in half a lifetime I recognised his smell immediately. It was Mystic Trev, and I was home at last.

Acknowledgements

Writing this has been a great pleasure, not least because it has put me in touch with lots of old friends. My old Aussie mates Trev, Steph Morgan and Kim were especially helpful, as were my grown-up kids, Dan, Jess and Harry.

My brother Richard and partner Trish, who are holed up somewhere on the Isle of Wight, read most of this in draft form and helped keep me going by laughing in all the right places. My brothers (Nick in New Zealand, Simon in Rio de Janeiro, Adam in Spain), and my sister Sue in Kirkby in Ashfield, all chipped in with their reactions.

To James and Lucy in Kirkby in Ashfield, Violet in the Netherlands and Christie in Spain – thanks for your input and for the regular demands that I get this finished!

Many thanks to Adam Crowther and the BBC Radio Bristol Upload programme for playing a number of these stories and to Richard Jones at Tangent Books for his support and encouragement. Thanks as well to Nicky Coates and Hilary Arundale for help in editing this book.

I must also mention Mike Manson who listened to bits of this without complaint.

I owe a real debt of gratitude to all these people but particularly to my wife Angie, who has had to endure the telling and retelling of this story as it has progressed.

Finally, thanks to the people of Rainbow and to the Silo Art Trail of Victoria.

Other Books by Jonathan Evans
The Mystery of Ernie Taylor's Abdomen

Jonathan Evans grew up in the Nottinghamshire mining town of Kirkby in Ashfield in the 1950s and 1960s and this collection of short stories brilliantly describes the hopes, fears and mishaps of young lads coming of age against a bluff East Midlands backdrop.

The stories capture a sense of wonderment with an adventure around every corner.

Jonathan displays a huge affection for his working class roots and the unusual characters who helped shape his whimsical world view. The combination of innocence, naivety and insatiable curiosity often result in hilarious and bizarre scenarios.

Jonathan is a popular reader at the *Let Me Tell You A Story Jack* spoken word events where the stories were described thus: 'His accounts, set against the backdrop of a Midlands pit village, conjure up scenes of characters and young conspirators dogged by trouble and misadventure. Every tale is spun with wit, grit, warmth and a wry smile.'

"This collection of tales will leave you feeling warm and nostalgic. Such a joy and a pleasure to read."
Adam Crowther BBC Upload

The Rum Jungle Hotel and other Travel Stories

When I wake up, I find myself in prison. Not your ordinary prison, but the sort that nightmares are made of………I'm beginning to wish that I'd gone to Benidorm. "

In the days before Lonely Planet made the planet a lot less lonely, Jonathan worked the bars of southern Europe before travelling overland across Asia and Australia.

This collection evokes not only the halcyon days of the hippy trail but of other places and people, from 1960s to the present day.

Jonathan tells of crocodiles, cyclones and revolutions, and weird and wonderful characters. He meets drug runners and accidental heroes at a time when we could travel the world simply by putting our thumbs out, and let the journey take us to wherever it wanted to go.

There are stories about exploding hippies, con men, shoot outs, the fabled mad strangler of Maungaturoto and even an episode involving Hunter S. Thompson's screen double.

Captivating, wonderful and enthralling. You'll never be able to predict what's coming next
Adam Crowther BBC Radio Bristol.

Hilarious! There's a whole world out there just waiting for you!
Mike Manson, author of Where's My Money?

Wild and witty, a blast of Gonzo on the overland trail. Get on board, It's a wild ride!
Word of Mouth.

Printed in Great Britain
by Amazon